HAMILTON'S BLESSING

HAMILTON'S BLESSING

*The Extraordinary Life and Times
of Our National Debt*

John Steele Gordon

Walker & Company
NEW YORK

Published by Walker Publishing Company, Inc., New York

All papers used by Walker & Company are natural, recyclable products made from wood grown in well-managed forests. The manufacturing processes conform to the environmental regulations of the country of origin.

Library of Congress Cataloging-in-Publication Data

Gordon, John Steele.
Hamilton's blessing : the extraordinary life and times of our national debt / John Steele Gordon.
p. cm.
Reprint. Originally published in 1997.
Includes bibliographical references and index.
ISBN 978-0-8027-1799-3 (alk. paper)
1. Debts, Public—United States.   2. Budget deficits—United States.
3. Government spending policy—United States.   4. Hamilton, Alexander, 1757–1804.   I. Title.
HJ8101.G67 2010
336.3'40973—dc22
2009044754

Visit Walker & Company's Web site at www.walkerbooks.com

First U.S. edition 1997

1   3   5   7   9   10   8   6   4   2

Typeset by Westchester Book Group
Printed in the United States of America by Worldcolor Fairfield

To Eleanora Gordon Baird,
to whom I am much indebted,
with love

The sinews of war are infinite money.

CICERO, *Orationes Philippicae*

*Annual income twenty pounds, annual
expenditure nineteen nineteen six, result
happiness. Annual income twenty pounds,
annual expenditure twenty pounds ought
and six, result misery.*

CHARLES DICKENS, *David Copperfield*

*A national debt, if it is not excessive,
will be to us a national blessing.*

ALEXANDER HAMILTON

*A billion here, a billion there, and pretty
soon you're talking about real money.*

SENATOR EVERETT DIRKSEN

CONTENTS

ACKNOWLEDGMENTS

My first thanks must go to George L. Gibson, the publisher of Walker and Company, who read my article in *American Heritage* on the national debt, saw a book in it, and persuaded me to write it. And when I had done so, he edited the result with great skill and tact, asking questions readers would want answered, playing devil's advocate, and deftly kicking the soapbox out from under me when needed. He has made this a much better book, and I thank him for it. Needless to say, any remaining faults are mine alone. Vicki Haire did a wonderful job of copyediting.

I would also like to thank Richard F. Snow, the editor of *American Heritage*, for commissioning the original article. It has been a great privilege to work for and with Richard, Fred Allen, Katie Calhoun, and Tim Forbes these last seven years. Not many people, I suspect, get the chance to make a living doing something they would happily do for free if they could afford to. But, thanks to them, I am one of those singularly lucky people, and my gratitude is boundless.

I am grateful to Steve Partenza and all the able, pleasant, and helpful people who work for him at First Response. When my barn had a serious fire and came within an inch of burning down this January, Steve—a contractor who specializes in repairing disasters, a specialty I didn't even know existed—stepped in and simply put everything to rights, leaving me with little more to do than choose the paint colors and indulge my native New Yorker's penchant for goofing off by watching other men work. I could not have finished this book on schedule without their professionalism and good cheer.

I must also thank Tom Schultz, who, after the damage had been repaired, took two disused horse stalls in the barn and, applying an apparent infinity of artisan skills, turned them into a beautiful and, even more to the point, functional office. For the first time in my life—although doubtless not for long—I now actually have more bookshelves than books. That, for someone like me, is not a bad definition of heaven on earth. Further, Dan Ferretti wired the place for electricity, telephone, and cable, and gave me exactly what I asked for: more plugs than I could possibly use. Thirty-six in one room, with a hundred amps will, I am sure, be enough even for this electronic-gizmo-loving historian.

Finally, let me thank the people at the North Salem Free Library who so cheerfully track down books and articles in the most obscure places with blinding speed and tolerate—with only the occasional richly deserved lecture—what is surely the town's, if not the county's, most egregious record of delinquent book returns.

John Steele Gordon
North Salem, New York
November 17, 2009

HAMILTON'S BLESSING

INTRODUCTION

IN 1790 A British journalist, searching for a way to bring home to his readers the size of his country's national debt, seized upon an image that has a distinctly modern ring to it. The debt, he wrote, is of "a sum which the human mind can hardly form an impression. Were it to be laid down in guineas in a line, it would extend upwards of four thousand three hundred miles in length."

At the time, the British national debt amounted to £272 million, a sum roughly as awesome in the economic universe of the late eighteenth century as the $11 trillion debt of the United States is in the early twenty-first. After all, at that time £500 a year was a handsome income, allowing its recipient to live a life of relative comfort; £10,000 in capital made a man rich in the eyes of his contemporaries.

The size and steady increase of the debt certainly invoked in the British population, or at least the small portion of it that then concerned itself with politics, the same queasy feelings the American body politic has had in recent years as we have watched our national debt climb to once undreamed-of heights. In 1700, at the end of the Nine Years' War, the British national debt had stood at only £16.7 million. By 1720 it had risen to £50 million. In 1748 it reached £76 million; in 1763, £131 million. The expenses of the American Revolution then increased it to £245 million by 1784.

Certainly the example of Spain was fresh in the minds of British political and economic thinkers. In the sixteenth century, Spain had been the greatest power in Europe. But despite the cash cow that was its American empire, producing, year after year, prodigious quantities of gold and silver, Spain was increasingly burdened by debt, and its freedom to pursue its interests by military or economic means was thus increasingly limited. By the end of the eighteenth century, Spain was barely clinging to Great Power status and, shorn of its empire, would soon sink to the level of a backwater.

But although critics of the debt had been forecasting the ruination of the British state for generations by that time, in fact British power and prosperity had been growing quickly throughout the eighteenth century. Before the Glorious Revolution of 1688, Britain had been no more than a marginal military and economic power, with only a few tenuous colonies in the Americas. As late as the 1660s, the Dutch navy had dared to sail right into the Thames Estuary, where it burned five British men-of-war and seized the *Royal Charles*, the British ship-of-the-line that had carried King Charles II home from exile in 1660. The British army at the time was of even less consequence than the navy.

Yet 100 years and £272 million of debt later, Britain had become the linchpin of European politics, the Royal Navy was supreme at sea around the world, and the sun had stopped setting on the British Empire. The British economy grew strongly during this period as well, with national income more than doubling (although, to be sure, the distribution of that income remained highly skewed toward the upper classes). By 1790 the Industrial Revolution—fortuitously born in Britain a few decades earlier—was rapidly increasing the rate of growth of its economy. It would, in the next half century, make Britain the modern world's first superpower, although the Napoleonic wars, which occurred at the same time, caused the national debt to further increase to no less than £844 million by 1819.

Clearly Britain's experience in the eighteenth century proves that the size of a country's national debt is not necessarily inversely correlated with its power and prosperity. Far from it. Instead, the British experience demonstrates that a national debt, properly funded and serviced, can be a potent instrument of national policy.

The secret, of course, is in the funding and servicing. Spain's debt had been in both form and substance a personal debt of the king, mostly owed to foreign bankers, who lent short-term. More, the tax system of Spain and the other major European countries was chaotic, arbitrary, and wildly inefficient, making timely payment of interest on the debt doubtful. It is estimated that less than half the taxes being paid by the French people in the 1780s, at the end of the ancien régime, ever reached the French treasury. The rest went into the pockets of the independent tax farmers who gathered them.

But Britain had turned its tax farmers into bureaucrats at the same time it had created a national debt in the modern sense, one funded largely by long-term bonds (and some, called Consols, that never mature) that could be traded in the marketplace. These bonds, in turn, served as collateral for loans to their owners. The effect was to greatly liquify the national wealth, allowing it to flow much more easily to where opportunity beckoned and to fund the costs of an expansionist foreign policy.

Thus no other country in Europe was able to match Britain's ability to marshal so much of its national wealth for the purpose of waging war, while disrupting its national economy so little. For instance, because of Britain's ability to raise cash, the government could hire foreign soldiers to fight many of the country's battles (such as the Hessians who fought in the American Revolution). This practice both overcame the disadvantage of Britain's relatively small population and kept domestic political pressure against an expansionist foreign policy to a minimum when casualties were high.

Such economic flexibility, as much as the strength of its arms and the quality of its generals and admirals, allowed Britain to end up on the winning side of so many wars, and to recover so quickly from the war it unequivocally lost, the one that brought forth the United States of America.

So is the current concern about the American national debt overblown? The debt of the U.S. government, considered as a percentage either of Gross Domestic Product (usually called GDP, it is the sum of the goods and services produced within our borders) or of federal revenues, is nowhere near as high as was the British national debt in 1819, the year Queen Victoria was born and when Britain was, in the words of the late historian Cecil Woodham-Smith, "within sight of the heights of power and of wealth from which it was, briefly, to dominate the world."

I think not. It is not that the size of the debt itself is the problem. A country as rich and productive as the United States can afford to service its present debt, just as Britain could afford its debt in 1819. After all, our debt was nearly twice as high, relative to GDP, immediately after World War II, when the nation stood on the brink of a vast economic expansion. Instead, it is the recent trend that is ominous. For that trend results not from a deliberate political decision to spend in deficit, but rather from nothing more than the sum of myriad decisions regarding taxing and spending that, collectively, now substitutes for fiscal policy. In a very real sense, the federal government *has* no fiscal policy, for the tail of political expediency has long wagged the dog of prudent policy in Washington.

Today, nearly everyone, conservative and liberal alike, agrees that something is terribly wrong with how the U.S. government conducts its fiscal affairs. Just consider. One has to go all the way back to the beginning to find a similar situation. The federal government was still in the process of establishing itself in 1792 and did not have a good year financially. Total income was only $3.67 million, about eighty-eight cents per capita. Outlays were $5.08 million. The budget deficit, therefore, amounted to fully 38 percent of revenues. The next year, however, sharply reducing expenses while enjoying increased tax receipts, the government showed its first budget surplus. Except during periods of grave economic or military crisis, the government would never again run up so large an annual deficit in terms of a percentage of total revenues.

Not, that is, until 1992. That year, the government of the richest and most powerful nation the world has ever known, facing no more than the ordinary problems that face any dynamic society in an era of profound change, had revenues of $1.076 trillion and outlays of $1.475 trillion, a budget deficit equaling 37 percent of revenues.

And 1992 was no fluke. The last quarter century of the nation's history has been marked by a doubling in federal revenues (in constant dollars) and the collapse of its only significant external military threat. Yet in those years the United States spent as much of tomorrow's money as it would have spent fighting a major war or new Great Depression, the primary causes of past deficits. That will have no small consequences if, tomorrow, the country actually has to fight World War III.

It's an old expression that "the time to save money is when you have it." And this was long thought to apply to sovereign states as much as to individuals. As Adam Smith explained in *The Wealth of Nations*, published the very year the United States was born, "What is prudence in the conduct of every private family, can scarce be folly in that of a great kingdom." In other words, Smith thought that governments should finance current expenditures out of current income, should save for a rainy day (or, more properly speaking, allow the people to do so by lowering taxes when the budget is in surplus), should borrow only when absolutely necessary, and should pay back borrowed money as quickly as possible so that it is available to be borrowed again when needed. And yet in the last seventy-five years, the United States has made no attempt whatever to pay down its debt and, more recently, has borrowed ever more money as though there *were* no tomorrow, despite the fact that most of those years were both peaceful and prosperous.

But if the modern spending habits of the federal government would hardly win the approval of Adam Smith, the great economist would be even more critical of the country's tax system, the other half of fiscal policy.

Because of the vast complexities of the modern federal tax system as it has evolved over the last century, corporations and individual taxpayers alike have no certainty whatever that others in similar economic circumstances are paying similar amounts of taxes, a fact that has generated vast cynicism. The tax code makes tax avoidance (which is perfectly legal and proper) easy and tax evasion (which is a felony) tempting. After all, if the best place to hide a book is in a library, the best place to hide a tax dodge (legal, illegal, or somewhere in between) is in the depths of a tax return the size of one or more phone books. This has made it nearly impossible to increase tax revenues relative to GDP. They have remained steady at about 19 percent for years, despite numerous attempts in recent years to raise more money to help balance the budget.

How did the world's oldest continuously constituted republic lose control of so fundamental a responsibility of government as its own budget? The answer, as with most governmental policy disasters in a democracy, is one innocuous step at a time. While politicians, economists—and many others—pursued their self-interests, the national interest largely got lost in the shuffle.

The budget system has become ever more heavily biased toward spending, while the tax system has become ever more unable to yield increased revenue. As a consequence, the national debt began spiraling upward, first only in absolute numbers, and then in the last thirty years, as a percentage of the gross domestic product as well (with a brief reversal between 1998 and 2003). Today it stands at over 80 percent of GDP, the highest it has been since 1950.

To put all of this another way: In the first 184 years of our independence, we took on a burden of debt of $300 billion, mostly to fight the wars that made and preserved us a nation, just as Britain took on massive debt to fight—and, of course, to win—the wars that made it a Great Power. In the last fifty, however, we have taken on more than *thirty-six times* as much new debt, at first in an attempt to maximize economic output, but in recent years for no better reason, when it comes right down to it, than to spare a few hundred people in Washington the political inconvenience of having to say no to one influence group or another. It is further proof, as if any were needed, that democracy, in Churchill's marvelous phrase, is indeed the worst form of government ever tried, with the exception, only, of all the others.

Today, the American debt has grown, a dollar at a time, to a point where, at $11 trillion, it is incomprehensible to the average American. (For the record, laid out in silver dollars, it would be about 273 million miles long, wrapping around the equator well over 10,000 times. The British debt in 1790, laid out in silver dollars—not that they quite existed yet—instead of guineas, would have gone around the world once.) In 1916 the richest man in the country, John D. Rockefeller, could have paid off the American national debt all by himself. In 2010, the entire Forbes 400 list could not pay off 15 percent of the national debt.

But far more important than the size of the debt or the cost of servicing it is its actual and potential effect upon the American economy and the national policy options that inevitably are

circumscribed by that economy. Thus the debt must be understood as the dynamic economic entity that it is, not just as a static
sum of money. As a historian I suppose I'm biased, but I don't
think there is a better way to achieve that understanding than by
looking at the long and colorful history of our national debt.

It's a very human story.

Chapter 1

THE HAMILTONIAN MIRACLE

THE UNITED STATES was born in debt.

Wars have been fought with borrowed money at least since Rome instituted the practice of forcing its richer citizens to loan the state money in order to help fund the conflict with Carthage in the third century B.C. The American Revolution was no exception on either side. This gave the British government one of its biggest advantages in the conflict, for with its well-established national debt and its efficient tax system it could borrow easily and, as we have seen, borrow it certainly did.

But there can hardly be a poorer credit risk than a newly formed government in rebellion against a Great Power. Such governments vanish with defeat, the leaders are hanged, and their debts become uncollectible. More, the American colonies had had only rudimentary tax systems, and the new Continental Congress, established in 1775, had none at all. The Congress was able to borrow something over $11 million from the French government and Dutch bankers—both countries soon went to war with Britain, hoping to take advantage of the situation— mostly for arms purchases in those countries. And Congress and the states sold bonds to wealthy patriots who were willing to risk the loss of their capital for the cause. But the money raised was not nearly enough. Thus the nascent United States had no choice but to resort to every financial expediency at its disposal in order to feed, equip, and pay the state militias and the Continental army.

The main source of revenue was, in fact, the printing press. Congress issued massive amounts of so-called continentals, paper money that was backed by nothing more than a declaration that it was legal tender. By the end of the war, these issues amounted to more than $200 million at face value. But this fiat money had quickly depreciated, as fiat money always does. Before the war ended, Congress had been forced to revalue earlier issues at only 2.5 percent of face value, and the phrase "not worth a continental" would be part of the American idiom for a century. Further, the state governments and Continental Congress used what were, in effect, forced loans, requisitioning food and supplies from citizens and paying for the goods with IOUs. These also quickly depreciated as they passed from hand to hand.

These expedients were effective enough to produce victory. But when representatives of King George III signed the Treaty of Paris, on September 3rd, 1783, and acknowledged American independence, the United States, while free, was in a state of utter fiscal chaos. The Congress was no longer paying interest on its bonds held by its own citizens. It had defaulted on its foreign debt and was months in arrears in paying the army. Worse, the new government that had been established under the Articles of Confederation in 1781, just as the fighting was ending, lacked any powers that would allow it to cope with the problem. It did not even know how great its total obligations were.

With the new state governments fighting for their lives against what they regarded as a distant tyranny, they were not about to cede any more power than absolutely necessary to a new and still distant central government, even one of their own devising. Thus members of Congress were chosen by the state legislatures and were subject to recall at any time, sharply limiting their political independence. Indeed it made them, in effect, ambassadors, not legislators at all.

To be sure, the new government had, in theory, exclusive jurisdiction over foreign affairs, but it lacked any power over foreign commerce, always a powerful instrument of diplomacy. And while it had the power to raise an army and navy, and to coin and borrow money, it did not have the power of taxation that would allow it to fund these activities.

Instead it had to apportion the costs among the several states according to the value of each state's surveyed land and wait for the states to forward the money. Thus the federal government under the Articles of Confederation more closely resembled the present-day United Nations than it did the modern U.S. government.

And as the United Nations has learned, asking sovereign governments (which invariably have pressing fiscal needs of their own) for money doesn't work well. Some states paid up promptly, others were soon seriously in arrears, and some, notably New Jersey in 1785, simply said no. The result was that the United States not only could not pay the interest on its debts, but could not even fund its current expenditures.

As if this were not enough, the American economy underwent a severe postwar recession as it adjusted to being outside the British Empire and finding its commerce barred from many of its old trading partners, especially the British West Indies.

The consequences of a federal government impotent to carry out its assigned duties were soon obvious. Foreign governments treated the United States with contempt. Britain refused to evacuate the forts in the Great Lakes region, despite the Treaty of Paris that required it to do so. It knew that the United States had no means to force such a retreat. Spain refused to recognize American control of the vast area west of the Appalachians and south of the Ohio River. Soon it closed the Mississippi to American commerce, hoping to induce the western population to shift its shaky allegiance in exchange for access to this vital waterway. And that allegiance was shaky indeed. As early as 1784, George Washington was saying that the westerners were "on a pivot. The touch of a feather would turn them any way."

The Congress tried to get the states to agree to a 5 percent tariff on trade with foreign countries. But any such change in the Articles of Confederation required the unanimous consent of all thirteen states, and this could not be obtained. Rhode Island in particular, long the center for smuggling on this side of the Atlantic, wanted no impediments whatever on its commerce. Calls for a more far-reaching reworking of the Articles were increasingly heard, including a plan for representatives of the various states to meet in Philadelphia in May 1787.

Finally Shays's Rebellion, a spasm of discontent by debt-ridden farmers in western Massachusetts in 1786, proved the catalyst for fundamental constitutional change. The rebellion was easily suppressed, but it engendered a powerful sense that the fate of the American experiment was hanging in the balance, that the situation needed to be addressed directly and immediately. This ensured that there would be sufficient attendance at the convention in Philadelphia to have a quorum. As it turned out, only Rhode Island failed to attend. And although the convention met for the purpose of making changes in the Articles, it quickly decided to write a whole new constitution instead. (Rhode Island would be the last state to ratify it.)

The document that the Founding Fathers created that summer in Philadelphia—the desperate poverty of the old government all too fresh in their minds—put remarkably few restrictions on the new government's power to tax, borrow, and spend.

The federal government is required to provide for such things as the post office and the census, which necessarily require spending, and Congress may not make army appropriations extending for more than two years. But it was empowered to provide for "the general welfare," a term left entirely undefined. By the late twentieth century it had come to be construed so broadly as to encompass even a museum dedicated to the memory of Lawrence Welk.

The new Constitution also gave Congress exclusive power over foreign and interstate commerce and the power "to lay and collect Taxes, Duties, Imposts and Excises," a very broad mandate. But it required that they be uniform throughout the United States, in order to prevent several states from ganging up on one or two rich ones, the same reason it forbade duties on the exports of any state.

To protect the interests of the less wealthy, the Constitution required that all revenue measures originate in the House of Representatives, elected by the people, rather than the Senate, whose members were to be elected by state legislators who were, in turn, overwhelmingly men from the top of society. But to protect those men of wealth, it required that "no Capitation, or other direct, Tax shall be laid, unless in Proportion to the Census." At the Constitutional Convention, Rufus King of Massachusetts wanted to know the precise definition of *direct taxation*. James Madison reported in his notes that "no one answered." It was a silence that would have no small consequences one hundred years later. Indeed, that silence echoes loudly to this day in the American tax system.

Finally, the Congress was given the power "to borrow Money on the credit of the United States," one of the very few major powers granted in the Constitution that has no checks or balances upon it whatever. In the context of the time, this was entirely understandable. The British Parliament, necessarily the model the Founding Fathers used in creating Congress, had come into existence at the end of the thirteenth century precisely to be a check upon the extravagance of the king, and remained such a check five hundred years later. Britain's richest men represented themselves in the House of Lords, while the merely affluent were represented in the Commons. The poor, having no money, weren't represented at all. So when Parliament voted to spend money, its members were, in a very real sense, voting to spend their own money. The Founding Fathers expected Congress to be no different, and, at least for a while, it wasn't.

Because the financial situation had been the most powerful impetus to the establishment of the new government, the most important of the new executive departments was certain to be the Treasury. It soon had forty employees to the State Department's mere five. And its tasks were as clear as they were monumental. The department would have to devise a system of taxation to fund the new government. A monetary system would have to be developed to further the country's commerce and industry. The national debt needed to be refunded and rationalized. The Customs Service had to be organized. The public credit had to be established so that the government could borrow as necessary.

All this was to be brilliantly accomplished in the first two years of the new government. It was, almost entirely, the work of the first secretary of the treasury, Alexander Hamilton. Among the Founding Fathers, Hamilton, because of his financial genius and despite never holding elective office, would have an impact on the future of the United States that only Washington, Madison, and Jefferson equaled.

But Hamilton was not like the other Founding Fathers. He was the only one of the major figures of the early Republic who was not born in what is now the United States. Instead he was born on the minor British West Indian island of Nevis and came to manhood on what was then the Danish island of St. Croix, now part of the U.S. Virgin Islands.

Further, he was the only Founding Father, other than the ancient and by then venerable Benjamin Franklin, who was not born into the higher levels of the local society of his native colony. Rather, in the brisk, if not altogether accurate, phrase of his political enemy John Adams, Hamilton was "the bastard brat of a Scotch pedlar."

Hamilton was certainly a bastard, but his father was not a peddler. He came, in fact, from an ancient Scottish family, being a younger son of the laird of Cambuskeith. But Hamilton's father was an utter failure as a businessman. He soon parted from his family, and Hamilton's mother was forced to open a small store to feed her two sons. Hamilton became a clerk in the trading concern of Nicholas Cruger and David Beekman at Christiansted, St. Croix, at the age of eleven or thirteen. (There is some doubt about Hamilton's birth date. Nearly contemporary documents imply it was 1755. Hamilton said it was 1757.) So bright and energetic was the young Hamilton—for his tainted birth had instilled a ferocious ambition to get ahead—that by the time he was in his midteens he was managing the concern.

Nicholas Cruger belonged to an old and powerful New York mercantile family, and he early recognized the talent of his young clerk. When he returned to New York in 1771 because of ill health, he left Hamilton in charge. Soon he helped his young employee come to New York to further his education including the study of law. Hamilton, still in his teens, left St. Croix in October 1772, never to see the West Indies again.

With the rapidly deteriorating relations between Great Britain and its American colonies, Hamilton threw in his lot with his new country. His immense talents and his capacity for work soon secured him an important role in the Revolution—as Washington's aide-de-camp—and its aftermath. When Washington became president under the new Constitution, on April 30th, 1789, he asked Robert Morris, known as "the financier of the Revolution" because of his success at finding money and supplies for the Continental army, to become secretary of the treasury. But Morris, intent on making money, turned him down.*

---

* It was a bad decision. Within a decade Robert Morris would be in debtor's prison.

He recommended Hamilton instead. Morris and Hamilton had been in correspondence for several years about the country's fiscal crisis and how to solve it, and Hamilton, still in his early twenties, had greatly impressed the elder man. As early as 1781, as the Revolution still continued, Hamilton had written Morris regarding the establishment of a proper national debt on the British model. "A national debt, if it is not excessive, will be to us a national blessing," he wrote. "It will be a powerful cement to our union. It will also create a necessity for keeping up taxation to a degree which, without being oppressive, will be a spur to industry."

Washington was happy to appoint his old comrade in arms, and Hamilton, now in his early thirties, gladly gave up a lucrative law practice in New York to accept.

Hamilton's background would always set him apart and give him an outlook on life and politics the other Founding Fathers did not share. It also made him uniquely qualified to establish the financial basis of the new United States. Far more than Jefferson, Washington, Adams, and Madison, Hamilton was a nationalist. Perhaps because he had grown up viewing the colonies on the continent only from afar, his loyalty to the United States as a whole was unalloyed by any loyalty to a particular state, not even New York where he spent his adult life.

Also, Hamilton was by far the most urban and the most commercial-minded of the men who made the country. He had grown up, almost literally, in a counting house and lived most of his life in what had already long been the most cosmopolitan and commercial-minded city in the country. In 1784 he had founded a bank that continues to this day, the Bank of New York, and would found a newspaper that also lives, the *New York Post*. Washington, Jefferson, Madison, and even Adams were far more tied to the land than was Hamilton. Jefferson, especially, longed to see the United States as a country filled with self-sufficient yeoman farmers who shunned urban life. Hamilton, at home in the city and deeply learned in both the theory and practice of finance, saw far more clearly than Jefferson how the winds of economic change were blowing in the late eighteenth century.

Hamilton was always to be, to some extent, a social outsider. Today we tend to think of the American Revolution as having brought "democracy" to the thirteen colonies. In fact it brought no such thing. The eighteenth century was an age of aristocracy, and the American colonies were no exceptions. Each colony had its oligarchy of rich, established families who dominated the economic and, under the control of a royal governor, political affairs of that colony. To give just one instance of how pervasive was the sense of social hierarchy: Students enrolled at Harvard at this time were listed not according to the alphabetical order of their surnames but according to the social standing of their families in the community.

With the removal of royal control, these oligarchies inherited a near monopoly of political power in each colony. Although the population of the United States in 1787–88 was almost 4 million, only 160,000—4 percent of the whole—voted for delegates to the state conventions to ratify the new Constitution, the most important political event of their lives. Even when only adult white males are considered, fewer than 25 percent voted. It was not for lack of interest. Rather it was that the right to vote was limited to those who owned substantial property, in other words, the oligarchs. That was precisely why the writers of the Constitution were so confident that Congress would be instinctively frugal.

The oligarchies, it need hardly be said, abused this monopoly of political power; monopolies, whether private or governmental, are always abused by those who hold them. The oligarchs often manipulated the legislatures to advance their own interests, such as suspending foreclosures for debt during the depressed economic conditions of the 1780s.* And taxes tended to be laid more heavily on those without the vote such as small farmers and laborers. It was the latter that had led to Shays's Rebellion in Massachusetts.

Although Hamilton married the daughter of Philip Schuyler, one of the richest members of New York's "Knickerbocker Aristocracy," he never fully belonged to it himself. While he could be charming, especially with women, he was too driven, too ambitious for fame and glory, too unable to suffer fools gladly, to be completely accepted by the men. They recognized his brilliance, utilized his intellectual and financial skills, but they never forgot where Hamilton came from or the conditions of his birth.

Very nearly Congress's first act was to set about devising a federal tax system. On July 4, 1789, it passed the first Tariff Act, largely written by Hamilton, and henceforth import duties would usually provide the bulk of the federal government's revenues until the First World War (although the proceeds from the sale of public

---

* That is why the members of the Constitutional Convention placed into the document a clause forbidding the states to impair the obligation of contracts.

land in the West, not a tax at all, increasingly contributed to the government's revenues as the frontier pushed westward).

But, at first, tariffs were not enough. To gain more revenue, Congress passed excise taxes on carriages, distilled spirits, sugar, salt, and other items. Excise taxes are internal taxes on specific goods or on the privilege of doing business, and the tax on carriages was clearly a tax on the rich (only the rich, after all, could afford carriages) but a very modest one. Virginia quickly sued, claiming that the tax on carriages was a direct tax and thus had to be apportioned among the states according to population (in other words, according to the number of people, not carriages). Hamilton, at the request of the attorney general, argued the case for the federal government before the Supreme Court. The Court agreed with Hamilton that the carriage tax was an excise. This, as it happens, was the first time the Court addressed the constitutionality of an act of Congress.

The tax on liquor might seem to be the first of the "sin taxes," but the idea of alcohol as "demon rum" was, in fact, largely a nineteenth-century concept. Instead, liquor, sugar, and salt were taxed simply because they were three of the relatively few commodities then manufactured on an industrial scale and thus amenable to efficient tax collection.

The federal government quickly ran into a serious problem with the so-called whiskey tax. In most areas of the country, liquor distillers were too few in number to effectively protest the new tax, and, in any event, they could easily pass it along to their customers in higher prices. But the small farmers in western areas were blocked from eastern markets by the Appalachian Mountains. They had to convert their grain to whiskey before it was in a valuable enough form to bear the cost of transportation across the mountains. A 25 percent excise tax was a heavy economic burden for them, and they flared into rebellion in 1794, the first direct challenge to the authority of the new federal government. The rebellion was quickly and easily suppressed, and the two rebels who were convicted of treason were pardoned by President Washington. But the point was made that the new federal government could, and would, enforce its writ.

A revenue stream in place, Hamilton quickly turned to refunding the debt incurred in the Revolution and by the old national government. Indeed there was not much choice for the new Constitution commanded that the federal government assume the debts of the Confederation. The argument was over who should benefit from this refunding. Much of the debt, in the form of bonds, requisition IOUs, and continentals had fallen into the hands of wealthy merchants in the major cities, who had acquired it at far below par (its nominal face value), some for as little as 10 percent of that face value.

On January 14th, 1790, Hamilton submitted his first "Report on the Public Credit," which called for redeeming the old national debt on generous terms and issuing new bonds to pay for it, backed by the revenue from the tariff. The plan immediately became public knowledge in New York City—then the nation's temporary capital—but news of it spread only slowly, via horseback and sailing vessel, to the rest of the country. New York speculators moved at once to take advantage of the situation. They bought as many of the old bonds as they could, raising the price from 20–25 percent of par to about 40–45 percent.

There was an immediate outcry that these speculators should

not be allowed to profit at the expense of those who had patriot-
ically taken the old government's paper at par and then sold it for
much less in despair or from necessity. James Jackson, a member
of the House of Representatives from the sparsely settled frontier
state of Georgia, was horrified by the avaricious city folk. "Since
this report has been read in this house," he said in Congress, "a
spirit of havoc, speculation, and ruin, has arisen, and been cher-
ished by people who had access to the information the report
contained, . . . Three vessels, sir, have sailed within a fortnight
from this port [New York], freighted for speculation; they are intended to purchase up the State and other securities in the hands
of the uninformed, though honest citizens of North Carolina,
South Carolina, and Georgia. My soul rises indignant at the avaricious and immoral turpitude which so vile a conduct displays."

Elias Boudinot of New Jersey, wealthy and heavily involved in
speculation himself, demurred. "I should be sorry," he said in reply, "if, on this occasion, the House should decide that speculations in the funds are violations of either the moral or political
law. A government hardly exists in which such speculation is dis-
allowed; . . . [I agree] that the spirit of speculation had now risen
to an alarming height; but the only way to prevent its future effect, is to give the public funds a degree of stability as soon as
possible." This, undoubtedly, was Hamilton's view as well.

James Madison, in the House of Representatives for Virginia,
led the attempt to undercut the speculators.

He proposed that the current holders of the old bonds be paid
only the present market value and that the original bondholders
be paid the difference between market value and face value. There
were two weighty objections to this plan.

The first was one of simple practicality. Identifying the original holders of much of this paper would have been a bureaucratic nightmare, in many cases entirely impossible. Fraud would have been rampant. The second objection was one of justice. If an original bond holder had sold his bonds to another, "are we to disown the act of the party himself?" asked Elias Boudinot. "Are we to say, we will not be bound by your transfer, we will not treat with your representative, but insist on resettlement with you alone?"

Further, to have accepted Madison's scheme would have greatly impaired any future free market in U.S. government securities and thus greatly restricted the ability of the new government to borrow in the future. The reason was simple. If the government of the moment could decide, on its own, to whom it owed past debts, any government in the future would have a precedent to do the same. Politics would control the situation, and politics is always uncertain. There is nothing that markets hate more than uncertainty, and they weigh the value of stocks and bonds accordingly.

Hamilton, deeply versed in the ways of getting and spending, was well aware of this truth. Madison, a landowner and intellectual, was not. Hamilton, in his report, had been adamant. "It renders property in the funds less valuable, consequently induces lenders to demand a higher premium for what they lend, and produces every other inconvenience of a bad state of public credit."

Hamilton was anxious to establish the ability of the U.S. government to borrow when necessary. But he was also anxious to establish a well-funded and secure national debt for other reasons, for he was fully aware of the British experience with its national debt. Perhaps the greatest problem of the American economy at this time was a lack of liquid capital, which is to say, capital available for investment. Hamilton wanted to use the national debt to create a larger and more flexible money supply. Banks holding government bonds, he argued, could issue bank notes backed by them. He knew also that government bonds could serve as collateral for bank loans, multiplying the available capital, and that they would attract still more capital from Europe.

But there were still many people who failed to grasp the power of a national debt, properly funded and serviced, to bring prosperity to a national economy. John Adams, hardly stupid, was one. "Every dollar of a bank bill that is issued beyond the quantity of gold and silver in the vaults," he wrote, "represents nothing, and is therefore a cheat upon somebody."

Hamilton's reasoning eventually prevailed over Madison's, although not without a great deal of rhetoric. Hamilton's father-in-law, Philip Schuyler, by this time a senator from New York, owned more than $60,000 worth of government securities, a small fortune by the standards of the day. It was said that listening to the opposition speakers in the Senate made his hair stand "on end as if the Indians had fired at him." Rhetoric or no, the House passed Hamilton's funding proposals 36–13.

The second major part of Hamilton's program was for the new federal government to assume the debts that the individual states had incurred during the Revolutionary War. Hamilton thought these debts amounted to $25 million, although no one really knew for sure. It eventually turned out that only about $18 million in state bonds remained in circulation.

Again, opinion was sharply divided. Those states, such as Virginia, that had redeemed most of their bonds were adamantly opposed to assumption. Needless to say, those states, like the New England ones, that had not were all in favor of it. Financial speculators, hoping for a rise to par of bonds they had bought at deep discount, also favored the federal government assuming the state debts. But land speculators were opposed. Many states allowed public lands to be purchased with state bonds at face value, even when the bonds were selling in the open market for much less. Any rise in the price of bonds would increase the cost of land.

Madison and others argued that it was simply unfair for Virginians, who had nearly liquidated their state's bonded indebtedness, to pay all over again for the debts incurred by other states that had not. "Where, I again demand," thundered James Jackson of Georgia, "is the justice of compelling a State which has taxed her citizens for the sinking of her debt, to pay another proportion, not of her own, but the debts of other States, which have made no exertions whatever?"

Fisher Ames, a congressman from Massachusetts, argued that since the new Constitution gave all revenues from tariffs—the best and surest source of funds with which to pay the interest on the bonds—to the federal government, the federal government should now assume the debt. "Let the debts follow the funds," he demanded.

In the middle of April 1790, the House voted down Hamilton's proposal 31–29. Four more times it was voted down, each time by so narrow a margin that Hamilton had hopes of making a deal. He had to do something, for he had tied the funding of the old national debt and the assumption of the state debt into one bill. Many thought that the state debt issue was "a millstone about the neck of the whole system which must finally sink it."

Hamilton might have abandoned his effort to fund the state

debts, but he had still one more reason for extinguishing as much state paper as possible and replacing it with federal bonds. The debts, of course, were largely held by the prosperous men of business, commerce, and agriculture—the oligarchs, in other words. These men's loyalties lay mainly with their respective states and the cozy local societies in which they had grown up. Although they had largely supported the creation of the new Union, Hamilton had every reason to suppose that their support would quickly fade away if their self-interest dictated it.

Hamilton, therefore, was anxious to make it in the self-interest of these men to continue their support of the Union. If they had a large share of their assets held in federal bonds, they would have powerful incentives for wishing the Union well. So he was willing to throw a very large bargaining chip onto the table to save his funding and assumption scheme. The new federal government had come into existence in New York City, and Hamilton, as well as nearly every other New Yorker, was hoping that the city would become the permanent capital. Certainly the city had gone to a lot of trouble to spruce itself up, spending £18,000 in the process (these pounds were in New York currency, to be sure, not in the far more valuable sterling.)*

Hamilton knew perfectly well that every state wanted the capital, and that Jefferson and Madison especially wanted the capital

---

* The dollar would largely replace the myriad other forms of currency in the 1790s, as the new federal government began to mint coins. Much old nomenclatural usage remained, however. An eighth of a dollar, twelve and a half cents, was known as a shilling until nearly the middle of the nineteenth century, despite the fact that the government never minted a coin of that denomination.

located in the rural South, away from what they regarded as the commerce and corruption of the cities. Hamilton intercepted Jefferson outside President Washington's Broadway mansion one day shortly after the bill's defeat and asked for help on getting his bill through Congress. Jefferson, who had opposed the adoption of the Constitution itself, and favored the states in nearly all federal-state disputes over the distribution of power, was opposed to the bill.

Nonetheless, he offered to meet Hamilton the following night for dinner, with Madison in attendance. There a deal was made. Enough votes would be switched to ensure passage of Hamilton's bill, in return for which Hamilton would throw his support to having the new capital located on the muddy and fever-ridden banks of the Potomac. To ensure Pennsylvania's cooperation, the temporary capital was to be moved to Philadelphia for ten years.*

The deal was made, and the bill was passed and signed into law by President Washington. Hamilton was right that the bonds would find acceptance in the marketplace, and the entire issue sold out in only a few weeks. The new government, with a monopoly on customs duties and possessing the power to tax elsewhere, was simply a much better credit risk than the old government and the states had been. When it became clear that the U.S. government would be able to pay the interest due on these bonds, they quickly became sought after in Europe, just as Hamilton had hoped, especially after

---

*Historians should probably be required to swear a solemn oath never to play the game of "what if." Still, one can hardly help speculating on how profoundly different would have been the history of this country, not to mention the history of New York City, if its political capital had been located in the city that so swiftly became its financial, commercial, and cultural capital as well.

the outbreak of the war in which the other European powers tried to reverse the tide of the French Revolution.

The third major portion of Hamilton's program was the creation of a central bank, modeled after the Bank of England. Hamilton saw it as an instrument of fiscal efficiency, economic regulation, and money creation. Jefferson saw it as another giveaway to the rich and as a potential instrument of tyranny. Furthermore, Jefferson and Madison thought it was patently unconstitutional for the federal government to establish a bank, for the Constitution nowhere gives the federal government the explicit power to charter a bank or, for that matter, any other corporation.

There are three main purposes to a central bank. It acts as a depository for government funds and a means of transferring them from one part of the country to another (no small consideration in the primitive conditions of Hamilton's day). It is a source of loans to the government and to other banks, and it regulates the money supply.

The last was a great problem in the new Republic. Specie—gold and silver—was in critically short supply. Colonial coinage had been a hodgepodge of Spanish, Portuguese, and British coins, often cut into pieces in order to make small change.*

The lack of specie forced merchants to be creative. In the southern colonies warehouse receipts for tobacco often circulated

---

* Spanish reales, the monetary unit upon which the dollar was originally based, were called "pieces of eight" because they were often cut into eight pieces for this purpose. This is why a quarter is still known as "two bits" and why the New York Stock Exchange quoted fractional prices in eighths, not tenths, of a dollar until 1997.

as money. Hamilton knew that foreign bonds could serve the same purpose. In his "Report on the Public Credit" he wrote: "It is a well-known fact that in countries in which the national debt is properly funded, and an object of established confidence, it answers most of the purposes of money. Transfers of stock, or public debt, are there equivalent to payments in specie; or, in other words, stock, in the principal transactions of business, passes current as specie. The same thing would, in all probability, happen here, under the like circumstances."*

But the bonds, of course, were of very large denomination. There were a few state banks (three in 1790) to issue paper money, but these notes did not circulate on a national basis. Many business deals had to be accompanied by barter simply because there was no money to facilitate them.

Hamilton did not like the idea of the government itself issuing paper money because he felt that governments could not be trusted to exert self-discipline. Certainly the Continental Congress had shown none when it came to printing paper money, although at least it had the pretty good excuse of utter necessity. Hamilton thought that an independent central bank could supply not only a medium of exchange but the discipline needed to keep the money sound. If it issued notes that were redeemable in gold and silver on demand and accepted by the federal government in payment of taxes, those notes would circulate at par and relieve the desperate shortage of cash. Further, because the central

---

* It would be only after the Civil War that the word *stock* would come to mean a share of ownership, while *bond* would mean debt; in Hamilton's day the words were largely interchangeable.

bank could refuse the notes of state banks that got out of line—which would mean that no one else would take them either—it could supply discipline to those banks as well.

Hamilton proposed a capitalization of $10 million, a very large sum when it is considered that the three state banks in existence had a combined capital of only $2 million. The government was to subscribe 20 percent of this, but Hamilton intended the bank to be a private concern. "To attach full confidence to an institution of this nature," Hamilton wrote in his "Report on a National Bank" delivered to Congress on December 14th, 1790, "it appears to be an essential ingredient in its structure, that it shall be under a *private* not a *public* direction—under the guidance of *individual interest*, not of *public policy*; which would be supposed to be, and, in certain emergencies, under a feeble or too sanguine administration, would really be, liable to being too much influenced by *public necessity*." In other words, Hamilton did not believe that politicians could be trusted with the power to print money, whereas a privately held bank could, because its owners would go broke if they printed excessive amounts. The history of many countries, including, in his own time, France under the First Republic, would prove him right.

To make sure that the private owners of the bank did not pursue private interests at public expense, Hamilton wanted the bank's charter to require that its notes be redeemable in specie, that 20 percent of the seats on the board of directors be held by government appointees, and that the secretary of the treasury would have the right to inspect the books at any time.

There was little political discussion of the bank outside of Congress, which passed Hamilton's bill, the two houses splitting cleanly along sectional lines. Only one congressman from states north of Maryland voted against it, and only three from states south of Maryland voted for it.

Hamilton thought the bank was a fait accompli, but he had not reckoned on Thomas Jefferson and James Madison. Jefferson, the lover of rural virtues, had a deep, almost visceral hatred of banks, which he thought the epitome of all that was urban. "I have ever been the enemy of banks," he wrote years later to John Adams. "My zeal against those institutions was so warm and open at the establishment of the Bank of the U.S. that I was derided as a Maniac by the tribe of bank-mongers, who were seeking to filch from the public their swindling, and barren gains."*

Jefferson and Madison, along with their fellow Virginian Edmund Randolph, the attorney general, wrote opinions for President Washington that the bank bill was unconstitutional. Their arguments revolved around the so-called necessary and proper clause, giving Congress the power to pass laws "necessary and proper for carrying into Execution the foregoing Powers."

The Constitution nowhere specifically authorizes the federal government to establish a central bank, they argued, and therefore

---

*Anyone who doubts the influence of great men on history should consider how Jefferson's intense, even irrational hatred of banks has affected the history of the United States. The savings-and-loan crisis of the 1980s, 160 years after Jefferson's death, had its origins, in a very real sense, in Jefferson's passion. For that passion, articulated by one of the most articulate men who ever lived, greatly strengthened a fear of powerful financial institutions in his political heirs. This led to laws that favored many small (and thus weak) banks over a few large ones. Even today, when thousands of banks have merged and banking across state lines has finally become possible, the United States still has more banks than all the rest of the industrialized world put together.

one could be created only if it were indispensable for carrying out the government's enumerated duties. A central bank was not *absolutely* necessary and therefore was absolutely unconstitutional. This line of reasoning is known as *strict construction*—although the phrase itself was not actually coined until 1838—and has been a powerful force in the American political firmament ever since.

President Washington recognized the utility of a central bank, but Jefferson's and Randolph's argument had much force for him. Further, he may have worried that if the bank were established in Philadelphia, the capital might never make its way to his beloved Potomac. He told Hamilton that he could not sign the bill unless Hamilton was able to overcome Jefferson's constitutional argument.

To counter Jefferson's doctrine of strict construction, Hamilton devised a counter doctrine of *implied powers*. He said that if the federal government was to deal successfully with its enumerated duties, it must be supreme in deciding how best to perform those duties. "Little less than a prohibitory clause," he wrote to Washington, "can destroy the strong presumptions which result from the general aspect of the government. Nothing but demonstration should exclude the idea that the power exists." Moreover, he asserted that Congress had the right to decide what means were necessary and proper. "The national government like every other," he wrote, "must judge in the first instance of the proper exercise of its powers."

Hamilton's complete response to Jefferson and Randolph runs nearly 15,000 words and was written under an inflexible deadline, for the Constitution required President Washington to sign or veto the bill within ten days of its passage. Hamilton thought about his response for nearly a week but seems to have written it entirely in a single night. To read it today is to see plain the extraordinary powers of thought he possessed. Even John Marshall was awed by them. "To talents of the highest order," the great chief justice wrote, "he united a patient industry, not always the companion of genius, which fitted him in a peculiar manner for the difficulties to be encountered by the man who should be placed at the head of the American finances."

Washington, his doubts quieted, signed the bill in 1791, and the bank soon came into existence. Its stock subscription was a resounding success, for investors expected it to be very profitable, which it was. It also functioned as Hamilton intended and did much to further the early development of the American economy. State banks multiplied under its control—from 3 in 1790, to 29 by the turn of the century, to more than 100 a decade later.

Had Washington accepted Jefferson's argument and not Hamilton's, not only would the bank bill have been vetoed, but the development of the U.S. government would have been profoundly different. Indeed, it is hard to see how the Constitution could have long survived, at least without frequent amendment. Jefferson's doctrine of strict construction, rigorously applied, would have been a straitjacket, preventing the federal government from adapting to meet both the challenges and the opportunities that were to come in the future. Abraham Lincoln and Franklin Delano Roosevelt, for instance, would both push the Hamiltonian concept of implied powers very far in seeking to meet the immense national crises of the Civil War and the Great Depression.

Even Jefferson, once in the White House, would come to realize that strict constructionism was a doctrine that appeals mainly to those in opposition, not those who must actually exercise political power. Certainly he did not let the fact that the Constitution nowhere mentions the acquisition of territory from a foreign state stop him from snapping up the Louisiana Purchase from France when the opportunity arose.

Hamilton's financial program quickly, indeed utterly, transformed the country's financial circumstances. In the 1780s the United States had been a financial basket case. By 1794 it had the highest credit rating in Europe, and some of its bonds were selling at 10 percent over par. Talleyrand, who later became the French foreign minister, explained why. The United States bonds, he said, were "safe and free from reverses. They have been funded in such a sound manner and the prosperity of this country is growing so rapidly that there can be no doubt of their solvency." By 1801 Europeans held $33 million in U.S. securities, and European capital was helping mightily to build the American economy.

Less than two years after Hamilton's funding bill became law, trading in state and federal bonds had become so brisk in New York that brokers who specialized in them got together and formed an organization to facilitate trading. This organization would evolve into the New York Stock Exchange, and within a little more than 100 years it would be the largest such exchange in the world, eclipsing London's.

But Hamilton's program and its enactment had one great and entirely unanticipated consequence. It produced the first big political fight of the new federal union. It revealed deep and heretofore unsuspected cleavages in the American body politic. "When the smoke of the contest had cleared away," wrote Albert S. Bolles in his majestic *Financial History of the United States*, published over a century ago, "two political parties might be seen, whose opposition, though varying much in conviction, power, and earnestness, has never ceased." It still hasn't, and the American political nation can be divided to this day largely into Jeffersonians and Hamiltonians, those who look more closely at the trees of individual liberty and justice and those for whom the forests of a sound economy and an effective government are most important.

Jefferson never ceased to rail against Hamilton's program. His "Remarks Upon the Bank of the United States," published a few years after the bank was chartered, is a savage attack upon Hamilton. Jefferson, for instance, considered only the inevitable inequities that had resulted from Hamilton's funding scheme. "Immense sums were . . . filched from the poor and ignorant," he wrote, "and fortunes accumulated by those who had themselves been poor enough before."

Hamilton, understandably, preferred to look at the results and felt abused. "It is a curious phenomenon in political history," he wrote in reply, "that a measure which has elevated the credit of the country from a state of absolute prostration to a state of exalted preeminence, should bring upon the authors of it obloquy and reproach. It is certainly what, in the ordinary course of human affairs, they could not have anticipated."

But by then, 1797, the political pendulum was swinging toward the Jeffersonians, and they would run the country for years to come. In the fullness of time, however, as the very few who were actually harmed by Hamilton's program faded from the scene and the very many who benefited, generation after generation, remained, it came to enjoy the praise it deserves. Of Hamilton's work Daniel Webster, with typical grandiloquence, would one day say "the whole country perceived with delight, and the world saw with admiration. He smote the rock of the national resources, and abundant streams gushed forth. He touched the dead corpse of the public credit, and it sprung to its feet. The fabled birth of Minerva from the brain of Jove was hardly more sudden or more perfect than the financial system of the United States as it burst forth from the conception of Alexander Hamilton."

Chapter 2

ANDREW JACKSON REDEEMS THE DEBT

I N 1792, A F T E R Hamilton's program had been enacted into law, the national debt amounted to $80 million, something on the order of 40 percent of the Gross National Product of the day.* As the government found its fiscal feet after 1795, however, it ran a deficit only twice until the War of 1812, causing the debt to shrink rapidly. The country's economy rapidly expanded as well, so the debt declined both in relative terms (i.e., in comparison to the size of the national economy) and absolute terms (its amount in dollars). By 1811 the total debt was only a little more

---

* The Commerce Department began officially calculating the GNP (the sum of goods and services produced in the United States and by American residents abroad) only in 1929, coincidentally just in time to allow the nation to watch it plunge into the abyss of the Great Depression. It has now been calculated by economic historians, with ever-decreasing precision to be sure, as far back as the 1860s. GNP figures for earlier years are educated estimates. In 1991 the government switched from reporting GNP to reporting GDP, the sum of all goods and services produced within the borders of the United States. The difference between the two figures is very small. The switch came about because most other countries report GDP rather than GNP.

than half what it had been in 1795 and as a percentage of GNP was far lower still.

Also helping to reduce the debt was the fact that in the late 1790s, after Hamilton had left the government, the ruling Federalist Party added many more taxes, including a direct tax on the value of houses, land, and slaves between the ages of twelve and fifty. It even passed a stamp act similar to the one that had helped lead to the Revolution. These taxes were intended to finance the Federalists' program of expansive government at the federal level. But, as economist John Kenneth Galbraith once famously remarked, while eighteenth-century Americans objected to taxation without representation, they objected equally to taxation *with* representation. And the Federalist taxes played a considerable part in the triumph of the Jeffersonians in the election of 1800.

In 1802, with Thomas Jefferson in the White House, the Democrats repealed all excises except the one on salt (which was removed in 1807) as well as the direct taxes on houses, land, and slaves, relying for revenue on the tariff, land sales, and the postal service, then running, believe it or not, a significant surplus. The government could afford these tax cuts, while continuing to reduce the debt, because American foreign trade was booming, greatly adding to tariff receipts. In 1790 imports had totaled only $22.461 million. By 1807 they had more than tripled, reaching $78.856 million. Much of this increased trade resulted from the effects of the European war that had broken out in 1792 and which raged for most of the next twenty-three years.

The war also caused the belligerents, especially Britain, to violate U.S. neutrality, seizing American ships and sailors. Between

1803 and 1807 the British seized no fewer than 528 American ships, while the French took 389 on various pretexts. In 1807 a British frigate went so far as to fire three broadsides, without warning, into an American warship, the frigate USS *Chesapeake*, when the *Chesapeake*'s captain refused to allow a search of his ship for British nationals. It was an indisputable act of war, and outrage swept the country. Had Congress been in session, a declaration of war would almost certainly have resulted. Jefferson knew that when Congress reassembled, he had to take strong action to head one off.

The result was the Embargo Act, one of the most extraordinary political acts in U.S. history. It solved the problem of foreign interference with American international trade by simply forbidding Americans to engage in such trade. The navy was deployed to enforce the embargo. In effect, in an attempt to get Britain and France to respect neutral rights while avoiding war, the United States went to war with itself and blockaded its own ports. Exports, which had been $48 million in 1807, fell to a mere $9 million the following year.

The immediate results were, at least in retrospect, entirely predictable. There was a political firestorm in New England and the Atlantic ports, whose economies were devastated. Smuggling became rampant; indeed it became so rife on Lake Champlain, which crosses the Canadian border, that Jefferson actually declared the area to be in a state of rebellion. And federal revenues, heavily dependent on the tariff, collapsed. In 1808, before the Embargo Act took full effect, federal revenues were $17.061 million. In 1809 they were a mere $7.773 million, and the government ran its biggest deficit ever, in dollar terms, up to that time. The lost revenues, as well as the political opposition, soon forced the repeal of the Embargo Act. It was replaced by the Non-Intercourse Act, which forbade commerce only with Britain and France, by far the two largest trading partners of the United States.

The Embargo Act was, in fact, an early form of trade sanction. Jefferson hoped, by denying them American products, to force Britain and France to respect American rights. But besides harming this country, the Embargo Act didn't affect the behavior of the European powers in the least. Indeed, it caused them to view the United States with contempt, a dangerous emotion to engender in international politics. When Napoleon seized Spain, in 1808, and put his brother Joseph on its throne, he also seized 250 American vessels and their cargoes in Spanish ports. When the U.S. ambassador demanded an explanation, Napoleon calmly replied—one wonders what the French word for *chutzpah* might be—that he was only helping to enforce the Embargo Act.

The United States drifted toward war. In the elections of 1810, many strongly pro-war congressmen and senators were sent to Washington, especially from the South and West. These so-called War Hawks were led by the very young Henry Clay, who was elected Speaker of the House. They used the cry of American rights on the high seas as a convenient means of whipping up sentiment for war, but their real objectives were the acquisition of land in the West that was then under Spanish control, and the expulsion of the British from Canada. So little concerned were they in fact with freedom of navigation that they even voted to reduce naval expenditures. New Englanders, meanwhile, busily making money from trade despite British and French harassment, wanted no part of any war.

But the most egregious act of the Congress elected in 1810 was to refuse to renew the charter of the Bank of the United States, due to expire in 1811, after twenty years. Jefferson had retired from the presidency in 1809, but philosophical sentiment against the bank was still strong among his political allies. A more compelling reason to oppose rechartering the bank for many of them, however, was the fact that more than 100 state banks had come into existence since the BUS had been established. These banks now heavily influenced state politics, and many of them chafed under the discipline of the federally chartered bank. Also, of course, it represented competition as well as discipline, for the state banks longed to take over the function of depositories for government funds, which would allow them to expand their bank note issues and thus their loan business.

Like Jefferson, James Madison had strongly opposed the BUS's original charter, but when he became president, he recognized its virtues. The Bank of the United States had functioned just as Hamilton had prophesied it would, as an effective fiscal and monetary mechanism as well as regulator of the American banking system. Madison instructed his Swiss-born secretary of the treasury, Albert Gallatin, to press for a renewal of the charter.

On January 24th, 1811, the House, by a single vote, rejected a preliminary motion on the bank charter, and the fight moved to the Senate. There, on February 20th, the Senate tied 17–17 on another preliminary matter, and Vice President George Clinton, in perhaps the only significant independent act by a vice president in American history, voted against the bank. The Bank of the United States was dead.

In ordinary times, this might have been just one more example of the shortsighted politics that is so often the price of democracy. But many of the men who voted to kill the bank were the very same men who advocated war—the most expensive of all public policies—with one of the strongest military powers on earth. Given the fact that the bank was the government's principal mechanism for collecting internal revenue and its only one for raising loans, the defeat of the charter was perhaps the most feckless act in the history of the United States Congress, although, to be sure, that is a title for which there has been no little competition over the years.

On June 1st, 1812, President Madison sent a special message to Congress detailing the many offenses of Great Britain against American citizens and sovereignty. He did not specifically ask for a declaration of war, but there was no doubt he would be willing to sign one if Congress so decided.

And Congress did decide on war, although by surprisingly narrow margins for so monumental and dangerous an undertaking— 79–49 in the House and 19–13 in the Senate—for New England remained adamantly opposed. Congress promptly increased army pay (from five dollars to eight dollars a month for a private) and provided very generous bonuses for enlistments, including 160 acres of land, an amount that was soon doubled.

But Congress then adjourned without raising taxes to pay for the war. The results, of course, were disastrous. By the beginning of 1813, while the United States had enjoyed several notable, if strategically insignificant, victories in single-ship naval engagements, it had found only defeat on land. The British had snapped up several frontier outposts in what are now Michigan and Illinois, but American attacks on Canada had all failed.

Worse still was the government's fiscal condition. Federal government outlays in 1811 had been a little over $8 million, typical of what they had been in recent years, and the debt was only $45 million. The following year, however, with the outbreak of war, outlays jumped to over $20 million. By 1814 they would be more than $34 million. Meanwhile revenues were adversely impacted as an ever-tightening British blockade sharply cut into tariff receipts. In 1814 outlays would exceed revenues by fully 211 percent.

Excise taxes on manufactured goods such as whiskey and salt, repealed in the Jefferson years, were soon reimposed, but the income did not materialize quickly enough to replace the lost tariff income or to fund the greatly increased military expenditures. Loans were needed, and quickly. The nation's financial markets—Philadelphia, New York, and Boston had the largest—were still in their infancy and unable to underwrite the large sums required. Besides, political sentiment against the war was strongest in these very port cities whose richest citizens were best able to loan money.

Soon the Treasury was nearly empty. It needed an immediate infusion of cash or the war effort would collapse for no better reason than lack of funding. Knowing the fiscal situation in Washington, the British had spurned a Russian offer of mediation. They intended to win the war with silver bullets, a tactic that had often worked for them in other wars.

In February Congress authorized the Treasury to borrow $16 million, by far the largest loan the federal government had ever tried to float up to that time, and Albert Gallatin, the secretary of the treasury, designed the loan to attract small investors. They could purchase loan certificates in denominations as small as $100 and pay for them in installments over eight months.

The loan's subscription period was scheduled to close on March 13th, 1813, and the loan would go through only if fully subscribed. By that time the situation was desperate. "We have hardly money enough to last until the end of March," Gallatin informed President Madison on March 5th. The public, however, was discouraged, and the subscriptions fell far below hopes. Gallatin extended the subscription period to the end of the month and allowed himself five extra days after that to try to raise any additional money needed.

As Gallatin had predicted, by March 31st, 1813, the government of the United States, in the midst of a war with a superpower, was dead, flat broke. The Treasury maintained accounts in more than thirty banks, but the total sum of their balances was not enough to finance even the day-to-day operations of the government, let alone a war.

Worse still, the extended loan subscription had failed to produce much further investment. Treasury Secretary Gallatin had less than a week to find the more than $10 million needed to activate the loan and allow the government to operate. He had only one place to turn, the Philadelphia merchant and banker Stephen Girard, the richest man in America.

Girard had been born in Bordeaux, France, in 1750. His right eye was deformed at birth and sightless. Still worse, it was too large for its socket and bulged out, its pupil fixed in the outer corner, giving Girard a fish-eyed appearance. As a child he was, naturally, tormented by his contemporaries about it, and he would be shy and sensitive about his appearance all his life. Although at the turn of the nineteenth century, men in his position had their portraits painted as a matter of course, often frequently, Girard always flatly refused to sit for one, and there are no likenesses of him taken from life. Even those drawn after his death usually show his face in three-quarter profile, obscuring his right eye. And his private life was less than happy. He married but his wife soon went insane, living in an institution for years, leaving Girard childless and unable to remarry.

Girard's family had made their living from the sea for generations, and he himself went to sea as a cabin boy at the age of fourteen. By the time he was twenty-two, he had a captain's license from the French Merchant Marine. Two years later, in 1774, he settled in Philadelphia. After the Revolution, Girard quickly became active in the highly profitable China trade, and the ships of his growing fleet were soon known in ports around the world, their captains buying cheap here and selling dear there.

Girard's was a new type of wealth in this country—liquid capital. Earlier American fortunes had been tied up in land and slaves. But Girard had cash, lots of it, and he turned Congress's folly to his own profit in 1811 when he quickly bought the non-financial assets of the Bank of the United States. He reopened it under the name Stephen Girard's Bank (under the name of the Girard Trust it would become one of Philadelphia's most prominent banks), with no less than $1.2 million in capital. That was a very large sum for the time, especially when one considers that it was entirely his own money.

The situation that the treasury secretary described to Girard was bleak. Subscriptions to the loan had totaled $5,838,200, hardly more than one-third of the total needed to activate the bond issue. David Parrish, another wealthy Philadelphian, had arranged for a New York syndicate, headed by John Jacob Astor, to subscribe to $2,056,000, provided that Girard subscribe to the rest of the loan, a staggering $8,105,800, over half the total sum.

Girard, who had several serious disputes with the government stemming from the Embargo and Non-Intercourse Acts and their successors, was in the catbird seat and could have driven the hardest of bargains. Indeed Astor had done exactly that, demanding, and getting, a steep, 20 percent discount from their face value on the bonds he purchased. But Girard did not. He simply said yes, asking only that the Treasury deposit the proceeds of the loan in his bank until it was drawn upon, a condition that Gallatin was more than happy to agree to, and that he receive a commission of .25 percent to cover his costs in trying to get others to participate, for Girard intended to sell as much of the government's paper as possible.

He expected to succeed, for he knew that his credit was far better than that of the federal government. After all, he had far more ready money with which to back it up. And he was correct. Within ten days, he was able to sell $4,672,800 of the loan to the public, another part to David Parrish, and his final personal subscription was $2,383,000, still a vast sum by the standards of the day, when the annual nonmilitary costs of the entire federal government were only about $1.5 million.

With money once more at hand, the United States was able to fire a few silver bullets of its own, and the military situation began to improve markedly. By the end of 1813, Great Britain was anxious to settle this distracting little war at the periphery of its global concerns, and the United States was able to extricate itself with honor, if not victory, from a war it should never have entered into in the first place.

And although Jefferson's political heirs remained firmly in control of the federal government, they were chastened by the experience of the war. On April 10th, 1816, James Madison signed into law the charter for the Second Bank of the United States, which closely resembled its predecessor.

With the end of the war in 1814, the national debt stood at $127.335 million, a level it would not see again until the Armageddon of the Civil War. For when peace was reestablished, the government once again determinedly whittled away at the debt, running substantial surpluses during most of the next twenty years. By 1829 it had been reduced to less than $50 million. This rapid reduction, however, was greatly facilitated by a change in the politics of taxation.

All laws have unintended consequences. The Embargo Act and the Non-Intercourse Act had almost nothing but. Not only did they gravely injure American foreign commerce, these laws acted also as a prohibitive tariff. Imports, especially manufactured imports from Europe, were largely barred from the country, and local industries, already beginning to grow, prospered mightily as a result. Unfortunately, these new enterprises, once confronted with the threat of renewed trade with competing countries, immediately sought a real tariff.

In the first days of the new federal government, Hamilton had wanted to accomplish two objectives with the tariffs he proposed. First, of course, he wanted to establish a revenue stream that would both fund the operations of the government and service the debts acquired in the Revolution.

Second, he wanted to protect American industry from competition from foreign firms until it was efficient enough to compete on even terms with the established industries of Europe, especially Britain. This is why he wrote Robert Morris that the taxes necessary to fund the debt would also spur the growth of the economy. This latter intent is a classic example of the second purpose of taxation—the first, of course, being the raising of revenue—one that developed only in modern times. This was to affect the workings of the national economy; in other words, taxation for the purpose of economic engineering.

This is one of the rare instances in which Hamilton failed to fully perceive the effect of unchanging human nature on the intersection of politics and economics. Economic engineering is perfectly sound in theory. Now and then, it even works in fact. In 1864, for instance, Congress imposed a 10 percent excise tax on bank notes issued by state-chartered banks. The purpose was not to raise revenue—and it didn't—but to drive the state-chartered banks out of the currency business and thus end the economic babel caused by thousands of circulating currencies that ranged from perfectly sound to completely fraudulent. This the new tax immediately did, to the great, long-term advantage of the American economy.

But far more often, economic engineering requires a benevolent—not to mention objective—despot to succeed, and such despots, of course, do not exist in the real world. Any time economic engineering happens to benefit a particular segment of the population, as tariffs protect domestic suppliers and their employees, that segment will always work hard to maintain its benefit long after the original purpose of the tax has been served. In the push-and-shove of democratic politics, meanwhile, economic engineering has also, of course, often served as a splendid refuge for scoundrels, providing cover for political favors to the rich and powerful that have little economic justification in the first place.

Congress at first ignored Hamilton's call for protective tariffs because there were few industries to protect and they had little political influence. The people who would have to pay the tariffs—the American population at large—loomed far larger on Congress's political radar.

That situation changed radically after the War of 1812. By 1824 there were 2 million Americans employed in manufacturing, ten times the number of only five years earlier, and many of them were located in New England. American shipping, meanwhile, was stagnant or in decline. The traditional New England opposition to tariffs began to fade as the new American industries pushed for ones high enough to protect them from renewed foreign competition.

The New England cloth industry, for instance, demanded, and received, protection. A duty of twenty-five cents a yard was imposed on cheap cotton cloth, effectively excluding competing British cloth from the American market. Other industries immediately sought their own protective tariffs, and some succeeded.

Besides the shipping interests, the other great source of opposition to a high tariff was the South. With few industries, and ever more dependent on the export of cotton to the British market, the Southern planters wanted free trade. In these years it was the tariff, not slavery, that most divided North and South and threatened the Union. Under Northern pressure, the tariff rose steadily, and in 1828 Congress passed what the South—as always a major exporter of catchy political phrases—dubbed the Tariff of Abominations. This, in turn, led to the nullification crisis in 1832, when South Carolina declared that states had the power to rule federal laws unconstitutional, including the tariff.

A direct confrontation, and, quite possibly, civil war, was avoided only when a new tariff calling for gradually lower rates was adopted. After the crisis passed, the tariff continued to decline slowly until the Civil War began for real in 1861. But it remained far higher than required to fund the government's usual revenue needs, and the tariff, then nearly synonymous with federal taxes, was a prime cause of the Civil War.

When Andrew Jackson entered the White House in 1829, he determined as a matter of deliberate policy to use the surpluses generated by the tariff to rid the federal government of debt entirely. It would be an enterprise unique in the history of modern nations and one that arose far more from the personality and history of Andrew Jackson than from economic theory. Indeed, it would contribute in no small way to the country's first great depression.

Thomas Jefferson and Andrew Jackson were, by far, the most important influences on the Democratic Party before Franklin Roosevelt. And they both held unshakable beliefs in a small and restricted federal government, the wisdom of the ordinary people, and the corrupting influence of money. Curiously, however, they had reached the same place in the political spectrum by very different routes, for they were profoundly different people. It is hard to imagine Thomas Jefferson ever being involved in a duel; Andrew Jackson fought no fewer than three and avoided several others only when his opponents apologized or intermediaries patched things up to his satisfaction.

Jefferson was a philosopher by nature, a theoretician more than a doer, naturally at home in the world of thought. He was uncomfortable in the rough and tumble of politics, inept in business, and never wore a military uniform in his life. Jackson, on the other hand, while highly intelligent, was not an intellectual at all. He was a doer to his fingertips, one who thrived in the real world and thoroughly enjoyed down-and-dirty politics. More, he was a superb general whose military career had been capped by the great victory over the British at the Battle of New Orleans in January 1815. Unfortunately it was a victory that came too late to affect the outcome of the War of 1812, for the treaty of peace had already been signed.

Both Jefferson and Jackson believed in dispersing power away from those at the top of society and toward the ordinary people. Jefferson had arrived at this position by intellectual means. After all, he had been very rich and lived his life in the highest reaches of American society. Moreover, Jefferson, naive and even cavalier regarding money, died deeply in debt. Jackson, however, had been born poor and was left an orphan by the American Revolution while not yet in his teens. During that war, he had refused to shine a British officer's boots and had received a blow to the head as a result. It left both a permanent scar and a lifelong hatred of aristocracy. Still, he had no intention whatever of dying poor, and he didn't.

To work his way up in the world, Jackson studied law with an attorney in Salisbury, North Carolina. When he was twenty-one, in 1788, he migrated west to what would become Nashville, Tennessee. There, he practiced law and speculated in land, the quickest, if risky, road to wealth on the frontier. By the time Tennessee became a state (and Nashville its capital) in 1796, he had acquired large tracts of land while serving as a district attorney and judge. By the standards of the time and place, he was rich.

James Parton, one of Jackson's early biographers, wrote that "the secret of his prosperity was that he acquired large tracts when large tracts could be bought for a horse or a cow bell, and held them till the torrent of emigration made them valuable." But like most frontier land speculators (and not a few today), Jackson got involved in complicated deals that involved credit, his own and others. In 1795, in Philadelphia, he sold 68,000 acres to a David Allison, taking the latter's promissory notes in payment. He used these in turn to purchase supplies for a trading post he was establishing. But Allison's bankruptcy in 1797 rendered Jackson liable for Allison's notes.

This affair would haunt Jackson for the next decade and a half before it was finally settled in its entirety. And it would give him a lifelong horror of debt and the use of paper to finance, or even to facilitate, transactions. From this point on, to Jackson, real money was specie—gold and silver—just as it had been to John Adams a generation earlier. Paper money, and what in Jackson's own day would come to be called commercial paper, were fraud, and those who issued such paper, largely banks in Jackson's day, were perpetrators of fraud and corruption.

Jackson saw the paying off of the national debt as a way of

ridding the country of paper money—for federal bonds held by banks often served as backing for issues of bank notes—but also as a means of diminishing the power of the fast-rising capitalist class. As early as 1824, when he first ran for president, he called the national debt "a national curse" and said that "my vow shall be to pay the national debt, to prevent a monied aristocracy from growing up around our administration that must bend to its views, and ultimately destroy the liberty of our country."

Jackson had no objection to self-made men like himself who sought only their own economic advancement and contributed thereby to the increased wealth of the country. By "monied aristocracy," he meant the older fortunes of the Eastern Seaboard and those who dealt in "paper" rather than "real" wealth such as land and manufacturing facilities. For Jackson and his followers, the symbol of this "monied aristocracy" was the Second Bank of the United States and its president, the aristocratic and sophisticated Nicholas Biddle. Its charter would be up for renewal in his second term, and Jackson was determined to destroy it. Eliminating the national debt was no small part of that objective.

And to achieve his goals, Jackson was perfectly willing to sacrifice internal improvements, dear to the hearts of his fellow westerners, such as roads. He noted frequently that when the debt was paid off, there would be a large surplus in revenues that could be used to finance these projects. In place of roads, Jackson offered another vision. "How gratifying," he wrote in one message vetoing an internal improvements bill, "the effect of presenting to the world the sublime spectacle of a Republic of more than 12,000,000 happy people, in the fifty-fourth year of her existence, after having passed through two protracted wars—the one for the acquisition and the other for the maintenance of liberty—free from debt and with all . . . [her] immense resources unfettered!"

Jackson was as artful a politician as he was a soldier. Despite objections from politicians across the spectrum, Jackson campaigned for reelection on the platform of killing the bank and ending the debt and was resoundingly reelected in 1832. He began withdrawing government funds from the bank while continuing to pay down the debt.

By the end of 1834, he was able to announce that he had succeeded in paying it off. The last of the debt would be discharged, Jackson wrote to Congress in the State of the Union message in December that year, and the Treasury would have a positive balance of $440,000 on January 1st, 1835.*

Jackson left no doubt as to just how important he thought discharging the debt was, equating it with peace itself. "Free from public debt," the president wrote, "at peace with all the world, . . . the present may be hailed as the epoch in our history the most favorable for the settlement of those principles in our domestic policy which shall be best calculated to give stability to our Republic and secure the blessings of freedom to our citizens."

Praise for Jackson's action on the debt was widespread. Roger B. Taney, the chief justice, wrote the president that the extinction of the debt was, as far as he knew, unique in the history of nations. Indeed, if Chief Justice Taney's supposition was correct in

---

*Jackson did not deliver the message in person. Thomas Jefferson, a poor public speaker, had stopped the practice, and it would not be revived until Woodrow Wilson, a good speaker, did so in 1913.

1835, it is certainly just as true today, at least among the Great Powers. Jackson's achievement remains singular.

The Democratic Party, for its part, decided to take advantage of the fact that January 1835 was also the twentieth anniversary of Jackson's victory at the Battle of New Orleans. It held a banquet to celebrate the two triumphs, although Jackson modestly refused to attend, sending the vice president in his stead. Both events were clearly linked in the public mind, and not only because Jackson had been responsible for each. "New Orleans and the National Debt," the *Washington Globe* wrote, "the first of which paid off our scores to *our enemies*, whilst the latter paid off the last cent to *our friends*."

But Jackson's hope of a debt-free federal government lived but briefly. When Jackson began withdrawing funds from the Bank of the United States, he deposited these funds in selected state-chartered banks around the country, called, by Jackson's political opponents, "pet banks." These banks, flush with the government's quickly increasing surplus funds, and no longer subject to the discipline the expiring Bank of the United States had provided by refusing the paper of unsound banks, began rapidly to increase the amount of bank notes they had in circulation.

The greatly increased money supply, inevitably, caused an upsurge in both inflation and speculation. Jackson's actions on the debt and the Bank of the United States, in other words, had the effect of increasing the very things he hated most, speculation and paper money.

Wall Street saw its first major speculative bull market in 1836, and land speculation became particularly intense. Land sales, handled by the government's General Land Office, had been only a little more than $2.5 million in 1832 but reached nearly $25 million in 1836. By the early summer of that year they were running at nearly $5 million a month.*

Much of this land speculation was financed with the flood of bank notes that had resulted from Jackson's destruction of the Second Bank of the United States and his use of the "pet banks" to hold government deposits. In less than eighteen months the nation's money supply increased by an awesome 50 percent.

Jackson was horrified by this rampant speculation and, characteristically, resolved to do something about it. He proposed to his cabinet that the Land Office accept only gold and silver in payment for land (except from bona fide settlers buying parcels up to 320 acres, who would still be allowed to pay in bank notes). The cabinet (many of whose members were themselves deeply involved in land speculation) opposed the plan. Senator Thomas Hart Benton of Missouri (who had once dueled, and wounded, Jackson on the streets of Nashville but was now a firm political ally) advised Jackson that Congress (many of whose members were, at the least, equally involved in land speculation) would never stand for it.

So Jackson waited until Congress adjourned on July 11th and then issued the so-called Specie Circular as an executive order. Needless to say, it brought speculation in land to a crashing halt and caused a sensation throughout the country. Senator Benton gleefully reported that "the disappointed speculators

---

* This sudden rush to buy land from the federal government in the mid-1830s was, in fact, the origin of the phrase "doing a land-office business."

raged. Congress was considered insulted, the cabinet defied, the banks disgraced."

The Specie Circular caused a greatly increased demand for specie in the West, draining the East of much of its supply of precious metal, and led to hoarding there. Meanwhile, of course, it also caused land prices to fall sharply from their recent inflated highs, and this caused many defaults on bank loans collateralized by land, squeezing the banks that had been so deeply involved in the speculation. Worse, much of the government surplus that had been deposited in the "pet banks" was due to be distributed to the state governments, further contracting the issuance of bank notes.

All these developments, of course, brought the boom of the mid-1830s to an abrupt halt in the West. By early the next spring the contraction had spread east, and Wall Street experienced its first great crash, in April 1837. Philip Hone, a former mayor of New York and himself badly hurt, wrote in his diary that "the immense fortunes which we heard so much about in the days of speculation have melted like the snows before an April sun."

Soon the entire economy was deep in depression. But Jackson, with the luck and timing characteristic of great politicians, had retired from office on March 4th, 1837, just before the full brunt of the depression had struck. It would be his successor, Martin Van Buren, who would have to pay for the consequences of Jackson's policies: the most protracted period of continuous economic contraction in American history, one that lasted fully seventy-two months.

And because of the depression, the federal government's debt was quickly reborn. Revenues, which had reached nearly

$51 million in 1836, shrank to less than $25 million the following year. Until the depression lifted, in 1843, the government would have only one year of surplus, and the debt climbed back up to $32 million. The Mexican War then caused a further rise, to $68 million, higher than it had been when Jackson took office in 1829.

But while the United States was once more without a central bank (as it would continue to be until 1913), the financial demands of war were much more easily accommodated than they had been in 1812. The country, and its economy, had grown far larger in those three decades. And its financial system was much more mature. In 1812 the term *Wall Street* had denoted nothing more than a street in New York's business district. In 1836, however, thanks to its first great speculative boom, it became the metaphor for American financial power it has been ever since.

And it was during the Mexican War, in 1847, that Congress, for the first time, altered the practice of appropriating specific amounts of money for each expenditure it authorized. Instead, it empowered the Treasury to pay all interest and principal on the national debt as it came due, regardless of the amount paid out. This raised little comment at the time. After all, there was no choice about paying the money, if the ability to borrow at reasonable rates was to be maintained. And it saved Congress the trouble of passing a specific bill every year. But it also, of course, allowed congressmen to escape the political scrutiny that came from being forced to vote, every year, to spend the money.

For many years this was the only federal spending that was put on what a later age might call "automatic pilot." In the twentieth century, however, Congress would resort more and more to this device until it became one of the prime reasons the budget went out of control.

After the Mexican War, the peace and prosperity of the early 1850s, greatly helped by the California gold strike, allowed the debt to be cut in half by 1856, to less than $32 million. When a new depression struck in 1857, however, the debt moved back up until, at the end of fiscal 1860 (which in those days was July 1st), it amounted to almost $65 million.

Only two years later, the debt stood at $524.2 million and was rising at a rate of well over $1 million a day.

Chapter 3

ARMAGEDDON AND THE
NATIONAL DEBT

W HILE INDIVIDUAL BATTLES may be decided by tactics, firepower, courage, and—of course—luck, victory in the long haul of war almost always goes to the side better able to turn the national wealth to military purposes. That usually means the ability to borrow.

As it happened, the American Civil War was the first great conflict of the industrial era. Indeed it was the greatest military event in the Western world between the end of the Napoleonic era and World War I, fought on a scale previously unimagined and foreshadowing the desperate global struggles of the first half of the twentieth century. As a result, both sides confronted wholly new fiscal demands and had to seek new ways to finance them without wrecking their domestic economies in the process. The fact that the North succeeded in coping with expenses of this magnitude— and the South did not—played no small part in the eventual outcome.

Both sides confronted terrible financial problems from the first. The government in Washington had been operating in the red for the previous four years because of the depression, borrowing mostly short-term to make up the deficit. In December 1860, as the Deep South voted for secession, there was not even enough money in the federal treasury at one point to pay the salaries of congressmen, who had to wait for their paychecks.

At the outbreak of the war in April 1861, federal spending in all departments was running at only $172,000 a day, raised almost entirely from tariffs and land sales. Three months later, war expenses alone were eating up $1 million a day. By the end of 1861, the War Department's daily spending was up to $1.5 million. Confederate spending was less but equally unprecedented.

How could these incredible expenses be met? In both peace and war governments usually have only three ways to pay their bills: They can print, they can tax, and they can borrow. It was Salmon P. Chase, Lincoln's first secretary of the treasury, who had to decide what mix of these options to use, and his decisions would have long-lasting effects. Some of them, such as the income tax, are with us to this day.

Chase was born in Cornish, New Hampshire, into an already distinguished family with old New England roots. One uncle was to be a senator from Vermont, and another was the Episcopal bishop of Ohio. When he was nine years old, his father died and he was sent to live with his uncle the bishop. Chase would always be profoundly religious, but his uncle's hopes that he would follow him into the church were not to be realized. He graduated from Dartmouth in 1826, when only eighteen, and for a while ran a school in Washington, D.C. Soon, however, he decided on the law and after passing the bar set up practice in Cincinnati.

Chase was a tall, broad-shouldered man, handsome in his prime, and possessed of a first-rate mind. But he completely lacked a sense of humor, and his occasional attempts to tell a joke were usually embarrassing failures. There is no doubt that this accounts for much of his inability to fathom the essential nature of Abraham Lincoln, one of American politics's great masters of the funny story. Chase's nearly lifelong diary, while an invaluable if tendentious window into the inner workings of the Lincoln administration, is ponderous and didactic, just like its author.

Chase always regarded idleness as immoral, and early in his career as a lawyer he spent his time between clients compiling the three-volume *Statutes of Ohio*, which quickly became a standard reference work in the state. He also became more and more deeply involved in antislavery activity.* This opened the door to politics, where he quickly found success and always hungered for more. His personal ambition to reach the White House would, of course, greatly complicate his already complicated relationship with Lincoln during his tenure as secretary of the treasury and would be a major factor in Lincoln's unexpectedly deciding to accept, in the summer of 1864, one of Chase's frequent offers of resignation.

His personal life was marked by much sadness. He married three times, in 1834, 1839, and 1845, but was quickly widowed each time. Of his six daughters, no fewer than four died in infancy. His profound anguish at these events, often expressed in religious terms, is painfully clear in his diary.

He was elected U.S. senator from Ohio in 1849, and governor in 1855. He first ran for the Republican nomination for president

---

* Chase would be, in fact, the author of the last paragraph of the Emancipation Proclamation, invoking "the considerate judgment of mankind and the gracious favor of Almighty God."

in 1856 and was, briefly, a serious contender in 1860. But when, at the convention, his support faded, he urged his delegates to nominate Lincoln. Reelected to the Senate that year, he resigned to accept Lincoln's offer of the Treasury, where he faced, from his first day in office, problems of a scale no treasury secretary had ever faced before, not even Albert Gallatin.

Both sides in the conflict soon resorted to the quickest way for a sovereign state to obtain money: the printing press. In December 1861, Northern banks had to stop paying their debts in gold, and the federal government was forced to follow suit a few days later. The country had gone off the gold standard, and Wall Street panicked. "The bottom is out of the tub," Lincoln lamented. "What shall I do?"

Since 1821, when the Bank of England announced that it would, once again, buy or sell unlimited quantities of pounds sterling for a fixed amount of gold,* the world's major countries had been increasingly doing the same with their own currencies. The great advantage of a gold standard is that it makes inflation impossible. If a country allows too much money to be created, relative to goods and services, gold will begin to flow out of the country as foreigners come to prefer gold to that country's currency. The gold standard was in important ways responsible for the great growth in world trade in the nineteenth century, by allowing traders to calculate future costs and profits with certainty. The great disadvantage, of course, is that no country on the gold

---

* One ounce of gold was worth three pounds, seventeen shillings, and ten and a half pence, an amount decided upon a century earlier by Sir Isaac Newton, of all people, enjoying the perks of a largely no-show job as master of the king's mint.

standard can fight a great war for very long. Traders will always prefer the certainty of gold to the inherent uncertainty of the currency of a country at war and quickly drain the country of its gold supply.

Soon Congress authorized the Treasury to issue greenbacks, as the new paper money was called, and by 1865 there would be a total of $450 million in circulation.

Chase, a sound-money man, had originally opposed the issue of greenbacks and had reluctantly gone along with them only from sheer necessity. Still, he made the best of the situation. The presidency ever in his mind, Chase had his own portrait placed on the one-dollar greenback. With photographs in daily newspapers still years away, there could hardly have been a better way for Chase to familiarize potential voters with his image. But then, ten years later, Chase, now sitting on the Supreme Court as chief justice, ruled that making the greenbacks legal tender was unconstitutional—despite the fact that he himself had authorized and adorned them as secretary of the treasury. Needless to say, Chase was roundly criticized for his about-face.*

The consequences of issuing large quantities of fiat money—money that is money only because the government says it is money and not because it is backed by something valuable such as gold—are inevitable, and they were as well known to people then, including Chase, as they are now. After all, the experience with the continentals was still alive in the country's folk memory.

---

* This ruling would be overturned the following year, with Chase then in dissent.

First, Gresham's law—"Bad money drives out good"—comes into play. Gold and silver disappear into mattresses as people spend the fiat money rather than the "real money." Even the government recognized the monetary inferiority of the greenbacks. Although they were legal tender, and thus an individual was obliged to accept them as payment of a debt, they were not accepted in payment of taxes.

The second effect of printing-press money is that inflation takes off. With the printing press working, the money supply increases while the amount of goods and services money can buy does not. The $450 million in circulation was about 13 percent of total government expenses during the war, and greenbacks contributed substantially to the steep wartime inflation in the North, as prices roughly doubled between 1860 and 1865.

The creation of a second form of money also set off a wild speculative bubble in Wall Street as the value of the greenback in terms of gold gyrated in response to Union victories and defeats. In July 1863, just before Gettysburg it took fully 287 greenback dollars to buy 100 gold ones. The speculators were called "General Lee's left wing in Wall Street" in the newspapers, and Lincoln publicly wished that "every one of them had his devilish head shot off." But the opprobrium affected their speculations not a bit.

The inflation experienced in the North, however, was nothing compared to what the South suffered as a result of paying *more than half* of its bills with paper money. As early as May 1861, the Confederacy was issuing treasury notes that would only be redeemable in gold and silver two years after independence was achieved. During the war, the Confederate government issued over $1.5 billion of these notes, and the effect of this flood of printing-press money on the Southern economy was catastrophic. In the first two years alone prices rose more than 700 percent in the South.

To make matters worse, the government in Richmond was not the only one printing "money," for state and city governments also issued notes. Because the South lacked good paper mills and elaborate printing facilities, counterfeiting was both easy and widespread. By the end of 1863, the Southern economy had spun out of control. Hoarding, shortages, and black markets spread relentlessly, while support for the war eroded as living standards fell.

Confederate paper money, of course, died with the Confederacy, but the greenbacks went on and on as a powerful constituency quickly developed around "cheap money" and the inflation that is its inevitable result. This opened a deep cleavage in American politics, one that has been with us more or less ever since. Whether and when to return to the gold standard was, second only to Reconstruction, the leading issue in national politics after the war.

Debtors, principally farmers, wanted more, not less, paper money for its inflationary effects, while creditors (often collectively known as "Wall Street"), naturally, wanted "sound money." The latter eventually prevailed, and the country fully returned to the gold standard in 1879. Still, William Jennings Bryan was swept to the Democratic nomination for president in 1896 after his "Cross of Gold" speech, which called for what would have been a highly inflationary monetary policy. And there was a Greenback Party candidate for president as late as 1944.

The South issued so much paper money because its ability

both to tax its population and to sell bonds was severely limited. The North had an established treasury and revenue-gathering system, with bureaucracy and procedures already in place. The South had to start from scratch. That was no easy task amid the screaming demands of war. Worse, the South suffered from an economy notoriously lacking in liquidity. Southern wealth, in other words, could not be easily translated into money that could be spent on military power. While the South had 30 percent of the country's total assets at the outbreak of the war, it had only 12 percent of the circulating currency and 21 percent of the banking assets. The word *land-poor* would not be invented until Reconstruction days, but it already perfectly described the Southern economy as a whole in 1861. In the four years of the war, the Confederate government was able to meet only 5 to 6 percent of its expenses with tax revenues.

The federal government, in contrast, raised fully 21 percent of its total revenues by taxation during the war, netting about $750 million by this means. Obviously the old tax system that had relied on the tariff for revenue would not suffice. The first timid steps toward a new tax system were taken as early as August 1861, and in 1862 the Bureau of Internal Revenue was established. The ancestor of the IRS, it is by no means the least of the Civil War's legacies to this country.

The act establishing the Bureau of Internal Revenue also levied taxes on nearly everything. Excise taxes were slapped on most commodities, stamp taxes imposed on licenses and legal documents. The gross receipts of railroads, ferries, steamboats, and toll bridges were taxed. Advertisements were taxed. The tariff was sharply raised.

Also imposed, for the first time in American history, was a federal tax on all income "whether derived from any kind of property, rents, interest, dividends, salaries, or from any trade, employment or vocation carried on in the United States or elsewhere,* or from any source whatever."

The first $600 in income was exempted by the act. Income between $600 and $10,000—a very comfortable sum indeed at the time—was taxed at 3 percent. Income over $10,000 was taxed at 5 percent. Taxes had to be raised sharply again in 1864, when the top rate on income was doubled to 10 percent, while taxes on liquor reached two dollars a gallon, no small sum when it would have sold for about twenty cents a gallon untaxed. But resistance to the heavy taxes—and high taxes' inevitable handmaiden, evasion—were not widespread during the war. One of the natural principles of taxation, it turns out, is that the people willingly pay very high taxes during wartime.

The third means of raising revenues, loans, also worked to the advantage of the North, thanks to its large banks and to one banker in particular, Jay Cooke of Philadelphia.

Jay Cooke was born in 1821 in what would later be called Sandusky, Ohio, the son of a lawyer and congressman. He went to work as a clerk when he was fourteen and soon ended up in the Philadelphia banking house of Enoch W. Clark. In 1861, just as the war began, Cooke opened his own bank in Philadelphia, Jay Cooke and Company.

Cooke's younger brother, Henry, had close political connections

---

* The United States thus was the first country to tax its nationals living abroad. It remains to this day virtually the only one to do so.

with Treasury Secretary Chase and saw to it that his older brother got to handle a $2-million bond issue for Chase, a matter he conducted with great skill and even greater dispatch. Immediately after the disastrous First Battle of Bull Run in the summer of 1861, Cooke "put on his hat, left his office and, visiting the bankers of Philadelphia, in a few hours collected over $2,000,000 on the security of three-year treasury notes."

A few days later Cooke accompanied Chase to New York and helped the embattled secretary raise an additional $50 million from bankers there, pending the issuance of government bonds paying 7.30 percent interest.*

Fifty million dollars was a huge underwriting for the banks of those days, but a drop in the bucket compared with what Chase realized would be needed. The War Department, after all, was spending close to $50 million a month by this time. The national debt had stood at nearly $65 million on July 1st, 1860, and a year later had risen to nearly $91 million. Chase estimated that by July 1st, 1862, the national debt would be at $517 million, only $7 million short of the actual figure.

Since Andrew Jackson's destruction of the Second Bank of the United States, government debt had been handled by the Treasury quietly placing bonds with the major bankers and brokers, who either held them in their reserves or sold them to their largest customers, just as the $50-million issue had been placed. But clearly a new system was needed if the government

---

* The interest rate of these bonds, the so-called seven-thirties, was chosen, apparently by Chase, for no better reason than that they would pay two cents a day in interest for every $100 in face value.

was to raise the vast sums required. It was Jay Cooke who devised it.

Cooke was made the agent of the federal government to sell five-twenty bonds.* He had the Treasury offer the bonds in denominations as low as fifty dollars and accepted payment on the installment plan. He deliberately tried to involve the little guy and make him believe that buying government bonds was not only his patriotic duty but a good investment for his own future as well.

Although Albert Gallatin had used many of the same tactics fifty years earlier, Gallatin did not have available to him an invention of the 1830s and 1840s—newspapers of mass circulation. Cooke did, and used them to add a new element, advertising and publicity. With that change, Jay Cooke invented the bond drive, a major feature of every great war since. He also introduced hundreds of thousands of Americans to the financial world for the first time.

Before the Civil War far less than 1 percent of the population had owned any securities (such as government or corporate bonds or corporate stock). Cooke sold government bonds to about 5 percent of the Northern population. According to John Sherman, an influential senator from Ohio (and the younger brother of General William T. Sherman), Cooke made the virtues of these bonds stare "in the face of the people in every household from Maine to California."

Not content with advertising, Cooke planted stories in

---

* So called because they could not be redeemed before five years or after twenty; meanwhile they paid 6 percent interest, in gold.

newspapers. "Here is a letter from a lady in Camden who orders $300," ran one story called "A Day at the Agency for the Five-Twenty Loan." "There is one from St. Paul, Minn., for $12,500. . . . Near one of the desks is a nursery maid who wants a bond for $50 and just behind her placidly waiting his turn is a portly gentleman, one of the 'solid men' of Philadelphia, at whom you can scarcely look without having visions of plethoric pocketbooks and heavy balances in bank. He wants $25,000."

By May 1864 Cooke was selling war bonds so successfully that he was actually raising money as fast as the War Department could spend it, no mean feat for that was about $2 million a day at this point. Altogether, the North raised fully two-thirds of its revenues by selling bonds. The South, with few large banks and little financial expertise, could raise less than 40 percent of its revenues by this means.

Cooke's singular service in helping to fund the Civil War made him a household name, the most famous and prestigious banker in the country. So when Jay Cooke and Company suddenly and unexpectedly failed in September 1873, the effect on the country's financial system was titanic. The panic of Wall Street was so severe that the New York Stock Exchange was forced to close for ten days until the mess was sorted out. The crash marked the end of the postwar boom and the onset of a new depression, one that lasted until nearly the end of the decade.

Cooke's successful bond drive caused a breathtaking rise in the United States' national debt. In 1857, before the onset of that depression, the debt had stood at a minuscule ninety-three cents per person. Eight years later it had grown by a factor of eighty and stood at seventy-five dollars per person, a height it would not reach again until World War I. But because the North could throw so much of the cost of the war onto the future, which the South could not, its economy remained intact, able to pay the soldiers and manufacture the war matériel that finally overwhelmed the rebellion.

If Abraham Lincoln must always be given the credit for saving the Union, there is also no doubt that the national debt was one of the most powerful tools at his disposal for forging victory.

By 1866, the first year of peace, the national debt stood at a then-staggering $2,755,764,000, no less than forty-two times what it had been only six years earlier and equal to about 50 percent of GNP.

Once again, however, the emergency over, the government doggedly began to pare it down. It ran a surplus of 7 percent in 1866, and it would not have another deficit—through good times and bad—until the severe depression that started in the 1890s produced one twenty-eight years later. (However, the official national debt, calculated at the end of each fiscal year, appeared to rise in some years by small amounts because of arcane accounting technicalities.) By the 1890s the national debt had been reduced by nearly two-thirds in absolute dollars. As a percentage of the rapidly expanding gross national product, it declined at an even faster rate to well under 10 percent. By the turn of the century, the Civil War had been largely paid for.

During this period there was very little political discussion regarding the debt. The doctrine of Adam Smith that debt should be paid down as expeditiously as possible was still unquestioned. Rather, it was on the revenue side of the budget that the debate raged. By the time it was over, the country would have an entirely new tax system.

Although the people were willing to endure very high taxes during the war, peacetime was another matter altogether. Immediately after the war the cry for repeal of the wartime taxes became insistent. With military expenses quickly dropping, the problem, basically, was what taxes to cut. American industrialists, who had prospered greatly thanks to wartime demand and wartime high tariffs, naturally did not want the tariffs cut. Because the Civil War had broken the political power of the South, the center of opposition to the tariff, they got their way. The tariff was kept at rates far above the government's need for revenue as the North industrialized at a furious pace in the last three decades of the nineteenth century and became the greatest—and most efficient—industrial power in the world.

Of course, no matter how large, efficient, and mature these industries became, they continued to demand protection, and, thanks to their wealth and political power, get it. As Professor William Graham Sumner of Yale explained as early as 1885, "The longer they live, the bigger babies they are." It was only after the bitter dispute between Andrew Carnegie and Henry Clay Frick caused the astonishing profits of the privately held—and highly protected—Carnegie Steel Company to become public knowledge, in 1899, that the political coalition behind high tariffs began to crack.

And hard as they fought to maintain high tariffs, the industrializing states, where personal incomes were rapidly increasing, fought equally hard to cut the wartime income tax and then abolish it. In 1867 rates were cut to a uniform 5 percent on incomes over $1,000. In 1870 they were reduced again, and in 1872 the tax was allowed to expire altogether.

Before the Civil War there had been little advocacy of an income tax in this country, at least at the federal level, although by the war six states had implemented such taxes for their own revenue purposes. But once a federal income tax was in place, thanks to the Civil War, it quickly acquired advocates, as political programs always do. These advocates pushed the idea relentlessly, and they had some compelling arguments.

The indirect taxes, such as excises and tariffs, by which the government had been largely funded, are inherently regressive. That is to say, they fall harder on the poor than the rich because they are based on consumption. The poor necessarily consume a far larger proportion of their incomes than the rich do, and therefore pay a higher percentage of their income in these consumption-based taxes.

It was not only advocates of the poor who argued for an income tax to redress the balance, however. Republican senator John Sherman, no radical by a long shot, said during the debate on renewing the income tax in 1872, that "here we have in New York Mr. Astor with an income of millions derived from real estate, . . . and we have along side of him a poor man receiving $1000 a year. What is the discrimination of the law in that case? It is altogether against the poor man—Everything that he consumes we tax, and yet we are afraid to tax the income of Mr. Astor. Is there any justice in it? Why, sir, the income tax is the only one that tends to equalize these burdens between the rich and the poor."

As for the claim by the wealthier states that they paid a disproportionate share—New York State alone had paid one-third of the Civil War income taxes—Oliver Morton, Republican of Indiana, had a simple answer. "I should be very willing to exchange with New York and agree that we would take her incomes and pay her taxes. . . . They have to pay the income tax simply because the large incomes are there."

But as usual with taxes, it was political power, not equity, that prevailed. Representatives of seven northeastern states, plus California, who collectively had paid 70 percent of the income tax, voted 61–14 not to renew the tax. Meanwhile fourteen mostly southern and western states, which had paid only 11 percent of the tax, voted 61–5 in favor. Support of the income tax, in other words, was almost perfectly inversely correlated with its local impact. Politicians will always try to follow the advice usually credited to former senator Russell Long of Louisiana: "Don't tax you and don't tax me. Tax the man behind the tree."

But perhaps the decisive reason not to renew the Civil War income tax was that it was simply not needed for revenue. The traditional federal taxes, principally tariffs, more than covered federal expenses once the war was over and, indeed, rapidly reduced the Civil War debt. It was politically impossible to lower these taxes, so it was impossible to justify another federal law for revenue purposes.

Instead, the argument to utilize an income tax was basically an argument for *social* engineering, using taxes to affect the distribution of wealth, not to raise revenue. This is the third rationale for taxation, one that was developed only in the late nineteenth century and would greatly flower in the twentieth.

Like taxation for purposes of economic engineering, taxation for social engineering is intellectually valid in theory. Indeed, there is little doubt that imposing an income tax and using the revenues to reduce excise taxes and tariffs would have had both socially and economically beneficial results in the late nineteenth century. But taxation for social engineering suffers from exactly the same problem as that for economic engineering: Once in place, it is very hard to remove, even when circumstances and political perceptions change.

The nineteenth century was the golden age of theoretical social engineers as the left—a word that did not enter the American political vocabulary until the twentieth century—rose in importance with the development of the labor movement in the East and the Populist and Granger movements in the West and South. One of the earliest and most influential was, of course, Karl Marx, who was the first to advocate a steeply progressive income tax, in *The Communist Manifesto* published in 1848, in order to check the advancing power of the bourgeoisie and the wealth of the old aristocracy.

Henry George, who would nearly be elected mayor of New York, advocated a single tax, upon the value of land. Felix Adler, the founder of Ethical Culture, advocated a 100 percent tax rate on incomes above the amount needed "to supply all the comforts and true refinements of life." One can only wonder how that amount was supposed to be objectively determined. None of these schemes had the slightest chance of being put into practice in the nineteenth century that gave them birth. But many would come to haunt the twentieth, despite vastly changed social and economic circumstances.

Killed in the 1870s, the income tax did not make much headway in the prosperous 1880s, when the federal government was running up surpluses so large as to border on the embarrassing, sometimes more than 30 percent of revenues. But when the panic of 1893 swept through the economy, the income tax movement was revived. With a Democrat, Grover Cleveland, in the White House and Democratic majorities in both the House and Senate, the chances for a renewed income tax were suddenly bright.

New income tax legislation called for a 2 percent tax on all incomes over $4,000. This was a very different sort of tax from the one in place from 1862 to 1872. That tax exempted only the poor. This new tax exempted everyone except the very rich. Of the 12 million American households in 1894, only 85,000 had incomes over $4,000, well under 1 percent. For the first time in American history, a tax was seriously proposed on a particular class of citizens, a class defined by economic success. This cost the new tax the support of Senator Sherman among other moderates.

In the House a classic debate ensued between Bourke Cochran, Democrat of New York, and William Jennings Bryan, Democrat of Nebraska. Cochran, whose home state would bear the biggest burden, by far, of this tax, argued that it wasn't necessary. He thought that the tariff reductions contained in the same bill would result in higher revenues from that tax through increased imports.* Further, he thought that by imposing a tax only on the rich, the income tax deprived the rest of the country of the privilege of supporting the cost of government.

---

* This is a pure supply-side argument nearly a century before the term even entered the language.

Bryan, ever the soul of eloquence if seldom of economic logic, pounced at once. "Why, sir," he orated, "the gentleman from New York said that the poor are opposed to this because they do not want to be deprived of participation in it, and that taxation instead of being a sign of servitude is a badge of freedom. If taxation is a badge of freedom, let me assure my friend that the poor people of this country are covered all over with the insignia of freedom. . . . The gentleman says he opposed the tax in the interest of the poor! Oh, sirs, is it not enough to betray the cause of the poor—must it be done with a kiss? Would it not be fairer for the gentleman to fling his burnished lance full in the face of the toiler, and not plead for the great fortunes of this country under the cover of a poor man's name?"

Much of Cochran's argument, of course, was tendentious twaddle that richly deserved its fate at Bryan's oratorical hands. But Bryan's in turn was pure class-warfare rhetoric, a form of rhetoric that would bedevil and cloud the politics of taxation right up to the present day. Yet it worked then to achieve the immediate objective, as it has frequently since, and the tariff bill that contained an income tax passed both houses. Cleveland, who was well to the right of his party in economic matters, could not bring himself to sign it, but politics made it imprudent to veto it. So he allowed the bill to become law without his signature.

The opponents of the income tax, however, were not finished yet. An arranged lawsuit was quickly brought alleging that it violated the constitutional ban on direct taxes unless they were apportioned among the states on the basis of population (not income), something obviously impossible with an income tax. The case, *Pollack v. Farmers' Loan and Trust*, would prove the most contentious and emotion-laden of the era, far more so than *Plessy v. Ferguson*, which established the separate-but-equal doctrine in race relations in 1896.

Joseph Choate, one of the most distinguished lawyers of his time, argued the case to overturn the income tax, claiming it was a direct tax. He had a difficult task. As early as 1796 the Supreme Court had ruled, in the case challenging the short-lived federal tax on carriages argued for the government by Alexander Hamilton, that direct taxes were those taxes that *could* be apportioned among the states. In 1881 the Court had upheld the Civil War income tax (which had already expired) as an indirect tax based on this interpretation of the meaning of a direct tax.

With precedent firmly against him, Choate pounded his opponents. "The act . . . is communistic in its purposes and tendencies," he roared, "and is defended here upon principles as communistic, socialistic—what should I call them—populistic as ever have been addressed to any political assembly in the world." By the time he was through, he had predicted the end of the established order itself if the income tax stood, saying it endangered "the very keystone of the arch upon which all civilized government rests."

The Court divided 4–4 on the question of whether the income tax was a direct tax, Justice Howell Jackson being absent due to illness. Given the interest in the case, and the political consequences of the Court's decision, this would never do. Although Jackson was terminally ill, he managed to attend a rehearing of the case a month later. Jackson was strongly of the opinion that the tax was within the power of Congress to enact, which should have provided the fifth vote and carried the day for the income tax. But one of the other justices (probably Justice George Shiras, but the opinions were unsigned) then changed sides, overturning the tax in what Justice Jackson called "the most disastrous blow ever struck at the constitutional power of Congress."

The income tax was dead for nearly another two decades but became one of the holy causes of the rising left.

Chapter 4

THE TWILIGHT OF THE
OLD CONSENSUS

T HE LEVEL OF the debt reached its post–Civil War low in 1893, at $961.432 million. The depression of the mid-1890s then pushed it back up to over $1 billion, and it stabilized there for the next twenty years as the federal government began pursuing a more expansive (and thus expensive) foreign policy and built a world-class navy from scratch. In 1890 the U.S. Navy had been hardly more than a coastal patrol force. By the outbreak of World War I it stood third in the world, behind only the Royal Navy and the new fleet created at the same time by Imperial Germany. As a percentage of the fast-rising gross national product, however, the debt continued to decline sharply. In 1890 the debt amounted to 8.57 percent of GNP, by 1900 it was only 6.76 percent, and by 1916, it was a mere 2.54 percent.

Despite the sound fiscal condition of the government, the Democrats continued to advocate an income tax, and William Jennings Bryan would be nominated for president in 1896, 1900, and 1908. But the Republicans were the dominant party after the Civil War, and it was only a deep if temporary split in the GOP that finally allowed the modern tax system to come into being. The motivation behind the new system was fairness, but because of the law of unintended consequences, one of the results would be the national debt going out of control decades later.

By the turn of the century, the Republican Party, long firmly in the hands of the eastern industrialists, had a progressive wing building in the West. Then, in the very first years of the twentieth century, the Republican president, Theodore Roosevelt, born to the eastern establishment, moved sharply in the direction of these Progressives, and their influence grew quickly. In 1906 Roosevelt even advocated a tax on inheritances, with the social-engineering purpose of preventing the "transmission in their entirety of those fortunes swollen beyond all healthy limits." Mainstream Republicans were, to put it mildly, aghast. But there was no real threat to the taxation status quo until the panic of 1907 and the short-lived depression that followed. This caused government revenues from the tariff to decline sharply.

The panic had been one of a long series that had swept the American economy, roughly every twenty years, since the early nineteenth century. These panics were an ordinary artifact of the business cycle, but as the United States developed increasingly into a cash economy, the lack of a central bank increased their severity more and more. In a financial panic, the demand for money soars as people flee bank deposits and weaker securities and move into cash. But without a central bank to supply the sudden demand, a panic tends to feed upon itself as perfectly sound banks are forced to close when they are unable to liquify their assets fast enough to meet the demands for withdrawal.

When the new panic struck in 1907, President Roosevelt was

deep in the Louisiana canebrakes, happily slaughtering bears, and the secretary of the treasury lacked the authority to do much. It was J. P. Morgan, then at the height of his power on Wall Street, who, through sheer force of will and his awesome personality, saved the day. He flatly forbade the Stock Exchange to close, even though the interest rate for call money had soared past 100 percent. (Call money was the money brokers lent to customers who bought on "margin," putting up only part of the purchase price of the stocks they bought.) He raised $27 million in a quarter of an hour to see the Exchange through. And he found a way for the big banks to temporarily use their large New York Clearing House deposits in order to meet demand for withdrawals, keeping them open as well.

The panic of 1907 was a short one and had, as well, one salutary result. The political forces, heirs of Jefferson and Jackson, that had opposed the creation of a central bank came to realize that with the country now possessing the world's largest and most powerful economy, it was simply no longer possible to operate without one. They still disliked the concept, perhaps, but they disliked still more the idea of having the country's future prosperity rest periodically in the hands of a Wall Street banker, even one as honorable as J. P. Morgan. The result was the creation, in 1913, of the Federal Reserve, and the United States had a central bank again for the first time since Andrew Jackson had killed the last one seventy-seven years earlier.

But the panic also caused a shortfall in government revenues. During debate on the tariff bill of 1909, Representative Cordell Hull—later Franklin Roosevelt's secretary of state—proposed reenacting the income tax of 1894 to increase government revenue and, in effect, daring the Supreme Court to nullify it a second time. Hull's amendment did not pass the House, but then, ironically, politics conspired to change matters in the Senate, despite the fact that fully one-fourth of the senators were millionaires.

Democratic senator Joseph W. Bailey of Texas introduced an income tax amendment and gained support from some influential western Republican senators, including William E. Borah of Idaho, who were sympathetic to the idea of the rich paying as much of their income in taxes as the poor did. Leading the forces against change was Senator Nelson W. Aldrich of Rhode Island, a self-made multimillionaire whose daughter was married to John D. Rockefeller, Jr.

In the Senate, Aldrich managed to largely salvage the principle of a high tariff, although tariffs would be on a downward path until 1930 when the Smoot-Hawley tariff was passed to help fight the gathering depression. But while they held together on the tariff, the Republicans were now hopelessly fractured on the income tax issue. Aldrich looked to the new president, William Howard Taft, elected in 1908, to save the day. Taft, a gifted lawyer, would come up with an elegant solution to the immediate problem. Unfortunately, it would be one that has haunted the country ever since.

Like Salmon P. Chase, Taft grew up in Ohio and belonged to a family with deep New England roots. He was born in Cincinnati in 1857, went to high school there, and attended Yale, graduating second in his class. He then attended the Cincinnati Law School, becoming the third generation in his family to practice law.

A mountain of a human being, often weighing over 300 pounds, Taft would be by far the largest man, at least physically, to occupy the White House. But Taft was slow moving, sometimes lazy, and often procrastinating. In 1885 he married Helen Herron, "a woman," Taft said, "who is willing to take me as I am, for better or for worse." It would be a long and happy marriage and result in three children, but it would be Mrs. Taft who provided the family with much of its ambition.

Taft got involved in Republican politics and in 1882 was appointed collector of internal revenue for Cincinnati, a plum patronage job. Taft, a naturally honest man, was soon horrified by the demands made on him to place others in his department, and to fire those who already worked there but were of the wrong party or faction. He resigned after only a few months. In 1887 he was appointed to the Superior Court of Ohio to fill out an unexpired term, and he was then elected to a five-year term in his own right, the only time he was elected to anything, except the presidency.*

Taft was immediately at home on the bench, and he would always be at his most content as a judge, involved in public affairs but removed from the hurly-burly of politics, for which he had few gifts. He quickly distinguished himself as a judge, and soon rumors circulated that he would be named associate justice of the

---

* Ironically, Taft disapproved of electing judges at all. In 1912 he vetoed the Arizona statehood bill because the state constitution called for the election of judges. Taft said it violated the federal constitutional guarantee of a republican form of government. Arizona quickly amended its constitution, and a new statehood bill was then signed by Taft. Once in the Union, however, Arizona immediately restored the election-of-judges provision to its constitution, and there was nothing Taft could do about it.

Supreme Court by the newly elected president, Benjamin Harrison. But Taft, never naive, realized that this was only talk. "My chances of going to the moon," he wrote his father, "and of donning a silk gown at the hands of President Harrison are about equal." Harrison did, however, appoint him solicitor general in 1890 and not long thereafter to a federal circuit-court judgeship.

He served with distinction for nine years on the federal bench until President William McKinley induced him to resign in 1900 in order to take the post of president of the Philippine Commission, charged with pacifying the newly acquired archipelago and establishing American rule there. Living in the islands, Taft soon grew deeply interested in both the islands and their people. So interested, in fact, that he twice turned down offers by President Theodore Roosevelt of appointment to the Supreme Court—long his greatest ambition—in order to finish his work on the commission. Indeed, he accepted Roosevelt's invitation to become secretary of war in 1904 only because the Philippines were then still being governed by the War Department.

As secretary of war, he quickly became one of Roosevelt's most intimate and trusted associates, his solid, steady ways nicely offsetting Roosevelt's impulsiveness. When Roosevelt left Washington on his frequent trips, he often put Taft effectively in charge. He didn't have to worry, Roosevelt said, making a joke about his friend's size, with Taft "sitting on the lid."

Although he genuinely lacked any desire to be president, Taft allowed himself to be pushed by his family and by Roosevelt into running as Roosevelt's successor in 1908, when the latter decided to honor the two-term limit established by George Washington. He easily defeated Bryan, 321 electoral votes to 162.

Taft was far more conservative than Roosevelt, and he revered the Supreme Court, which he would finally, and very happily, reach when President Harding appointed him chief justice in 1921.* The idea of legislation that directly defied a constitutional ruling of the Court—such as repassing unchanged the income tax bill of 1894— horrified Taft. If the Court yielded, he thought, its position as arbiter of the Constitution would be gravely compromised. If it did not, it would be setting itself against the two popularly elected branches of government, and a messy political showdown would surely ensue.

Taft crafted a very lawyerly solution to the immediate political problem. He suggested avoiding a confrontation with the Court by proposing a constitutional amendment to permit a personal income tax. Then, to satisfy the mounting political demand for an immediate tax on the incomes of the rich, Taft called for a 2 percent tax on the profits of corporations. Since at that time stockholding was almost entirely confined to the very affluent, a tax on corporate profits was, it was thought, for all intents and purposes a tax on the incomes of the rich.†

Needless to say, the corporate tax was challenged, but in 1911 the Supreme Court ruled unanimously that it was not a direct tax upon income but an indirect tax, measured by income, on the

---

* Taft, therefore, is the only president to hold high public office after leaving the White House, although John Quincy Adams served as a congressman.

† Actually, economists cannot say exactly who pays corporate income taxes. For any given company it is some unknowable combination of consumers (who pay higher prices), employees (who receive lower wages), and the stockholders (who receive a lower return on their investment), depending upon the company's individual economic and competitive circumstances.

privilege of doing business as a corporation. In other words, it was an excise tax, not an income tax at all. One can hardly help admiring the legal artistry of Taft's deft end run around an inconvenient phrase in the Constitution. But his corporate income tax would turn out to be quite as persistent and pernicious as Hamilton's protective tariff, for it would cause the United States to have two completely separate income taxes, corporate and personal.

Meanwhile, the proposed Sixteenth Amendment to the Constitution, to allow a personal income tax, passed the Senate by a vote of 77–0 and the House by 318–14, with 55 abstentions, a remarkably high number on so grave a matter as a constitutional amendment. Doubtless, many who had voted for it or abstained counted on the difficulty of gaining the agreement of the needed three-fourths of the state legislatures. They were severely disappointed in that regard, however, and the amendment was declared adopted on February 3rd, 1913.

By then the split within the Republican ranks had torn the party completely apart. Roosevelt had broken with Taft at the Republican Convention in 1912, where the latter was renominated. He and the Progressives stormed out and formed their own party, under the banner of the Bull Moose, and took more than half the Republican popular vote with them. As a result, not only did the White House fall into the hands of a Democrat for the first time in twenty years, but Woodrow Wilson had solid majorities in both houses of Congress.

There was now no doubt that a personal income tax was coming soon, the only question was the details, where the devil, in politics, is usually found. That's why the great German chancellor Otto von Bismarck said that the two things you don't want to watch being made are laws and sausages. And the personal income tax law signed by President Wilson on October 3rd, 1913, was classic legislative sausage.

By far the most significant aspect of the law for the future of the country (and the debt) was the failure to merge the two income tax systems, corporate and personal. The corporate tax had been instituted only as a means of taxing the incomes of the rich. Once the Sixteenth Amendment made it possible to do that directly, the need for the separate corporate tax vanished. This could have been done, simply enough, by treating the earnings of a corporation, on a per-share basis, as the income of the stockholders and requiring the corporations to withhold the estimated taxes, just as they withhold the estimated taxes on wages. This is how the earnings of partnerships (as well as those of usually small, tightly held "Sub Chapter S corporations") are taxed, and there is no economic or logical—as opposed to political—reason for larger, publicly held corporations to be treated differently.

Indeed there are strong economic reasons for *not* treating them differently. For instance, passing the tax liability on to the stockholders would make it in the interests of corporate management to concentrate solely on ways to maximize pretax profit—which is to say, maximize the creation of wealth—for after-tax profit would no longer be a corporate concern. Today the latter is a great concern when the tax return of a major corporation can easily be a stack of forms six feet high (or would be if they were printed out), and exactly how they are filled out can mean a difference of millions in "take-home profit." Every large corporation has many dozens of accountants who do nothing but work on the company's federal tax returns.

But the corporate income tax at the time was viewed simply as one means of taxing the incomes of the rich and the personal income tax as another. The left wing of American politics, in firm control of the federal government for the first time, naturally had no objection to taxing the rich twice. Since the vast majority of the people were unaffected by either tax, there was little political pressure to not do so.

Because the taxes on corporate income and personal income have never been integrated, however, many perverse—and entirely unintended—consequences have resulted. One is that the interest paid by corporations on bonds comes out of pretax income—it's a deduction on the corporate tax return—but dividends on stock are paid out of after-tax income and then taxed again as personal income when received by the stockholder. Under current tax rates, dividends are taxed no higher than 15 percent, but will return to the rate on regular income in 2011 unless Congress acts.

Worse, as we will see, the rich and their advisers soon learned to exploit the interaction of the two systems to escape not only being taxed twice but being taxed at all. The lack of coordination between the laws of personal and corporate income has provided nearly endless opportunities for the lawyers, accountants, and advisers of the affluent (about half a million people now earn their living doing this) to find ways to shift income between corporate and personal in order to postpone taxes, pay the lowest ones possible, or avoid them altogether.

Politicians have also found the two separate tax systems very useful for the pursuit of their own self-interests. Those of the right have found them a very convenient arrangement for quietly handing out political favors to the rich and powerful through artfully worded amendments that sound innocuous but actually benefit only a few or even a single taxpayer, either corporate or individual. Meanwhile, the failure to merge the corporate and personal income tax systems provided the politicians of the left with a potent political straw man—"the corporations"—that they have been using with great effect ever since.

And although the personal income tax seems very simple in retrospect—the bill was only fourteen pages long—it already contained the seeds of vast complexity. There was an exemption for income below $3,000, thus allowing the tax to reach into the upper middle class, but there was also a marital deduction of $1,000. At those rates 98 percent of American families were exempt. A "normal rate" of 1 percent was charged on income above $3,000, but above $20,000 in taxable income, rates began to rise until they reached 7 percent on incomes over $500,000, a titanic sum, to be sure, by the standards of the early twentieth century.

To counterbalance these rates, however, there were many exclusions. The interest on state and local bonds was not taxed, for the Supreme Court had ruled that unconstitutional in the same decision that had outlawed the income tax in 1895. Gifts and inheritances were exempt. So were the proceeds of life insurance policies, giving the life insurance lobby the distinction of being the first of countless thousands to extract a favorable income tax proviso from Congress.

And there were numerous deductions as well. Business expenses, naturally, were excluded. But so was interest paid on all debts, other taxes, uninsured casualty losses, bad debts, depreciation of property, and dividends on stock (up to $20,000).

One aspect of the 1913 income tax, however, was better, from a tax-collection standpoint, than what we have had since. It was what is known in tax jargon as "deduction at source." Taxes owed on wages, interest, and dividends were withheld, and any excess taxes collected were refunded at the end of the tax year. In 1916, unfortunately, this system was replaced with "information at source," with companies and banks only informing the government of wages, dividends, and interest paid.

Wages were again subject to withholding during World War II and remain so, of course, but not other forms of income. The result has been a clerical nightmare for the IRS, which today receives annually more than 1 billion "1099" forms reporting income paid, which it has to match up with well over 100 million "1040" forms reporting income received. The opportunities for, the temptation to, and, doubtless, the incidence of evasion are vast.

In the beginning, however, the income tax caused hardly a ripple because so few families were then subject to it. Only 357,598 "1040" forms (as they were called even then) were filed in 1914.

Slightly over a year after the modern personal income tax was introduced, however, World War I began and modern times began with it.

The same fiscal pattern that had marked the Civil War repeated during World War I. Again, government revenues and outlays moved to a new, permanently higher plane, as they have after every great war in U.S. history. With the exception of 1865, the federal government had never spent even close to $1 billion in one year until 1917. Since that year it has never spent less than $2.9 billion.

And there were still only three ways to raise money to pay the extraordinary expenses of industrialized warfare. In the much more sophisticated industrial economy that had evolved since the Civil War, however, the use of the printing press to pay government bills was no longer practical. In any event, the power to print money was now vested in the politically independent Federal Reserve. This left only borrowing and taxes.

The debt, a trivial $1.2 billion in 1916, a level it had been at for twenty years, rose by a factor of twenty during the war, peaking at over $25 billion in 1919. With Jay Cooke's model to work with, a series of bond drives aimed at the small investor was immediately implemented. The publicity techniques, of course, were now much more elaborate, including the use of that brand-new invention, the Hollywood celebrity. Douglas Fairbanks, Mary Pickford, Charlie Chaplin, among others, gave much of their time to the selling of Liberty Bonds.

Taxes too were sharply increased to help pay for the war effort. Although the war caused an immediate and continuing jump in American exports, principally war matériel to the Allied powers, imports dived and the revenues from the tariff, derived solely from imports, dived along with them. By 1916, although the country was still at peace, the government, facing sharply increased naval expenditures as well as falling revenues, projected a deficit of $177 million by year's end.

The government turned immediately to the income tax to plug the gap because that tax had one powerful advantage over other taxes: It could produce increased revenue very quickly. As the clouds of war darkened during the Wilson administration, it turned to the income tax more and more. When the country actually declared war, in April 1917, the exemption on income taxes was dropped from $3,000 to $1,000 ($2,000 for married couples), thus embracing much of the middle class just as the Civil War income tax had. The normal tax rate was doubled to 2 percent, and surtaxes ranged all the way up to 40 percent. They would be at 77 percent by war's end. Federal revenues soared from $1.1 billion in 1917 to $3.6 billion the following year. As always in wartime, there was little public objection to the sharply raised taxes.

This, of course, changed the nature of the federal tax system. In 1910 tariff and excise taxes had provided over 90 percent of federal revenues. Today they provide well under 10 percent. In 1913 the income tax was a mere amendment to a tariff bill, a social-engineering device to force the rich to pay "their fair share." By 1920 it dominated the federal tax structure and has ever since. Today only Social Security taxes come close to providing as great a share of federal revenue.

And with the federal government's main source of revenue being an income tax that featured highly progressive marginal rates—which is to say, the higher one's income, the higher the tax rate on the last dollar earned—the whole basis of tax debate in this country shifted. When the tariff and excise taxes had been dominant, the debate, beyond the basic question of how much revenue should be raised, was between specific groups of producers and consumers and between regions of the country. Both textile workers and their employers in New England, for instance, benefited from high tariffs on cotton cloth, whereas sharecroppers and their landlords in the South benefited from low ones. With the income tax, the debate was now between economic classes.* It is ironic that in the most un-Marxist country on earth, so central an issue as taxation should have to be fought out using a basically Marxist vision of society. But that is the case. In the 1930s even the nation's affluent were, presumably quite unconsciously, using a Marxist worldview when they described Franklin Roosevelt as "a traitor to his class."

To close the 1916 deficit, for instance, President Wilson wanted to lower the personal exemption of the income tax, which would have brought more families under the tax. The House voted instead to raise the normal rate from 1 percent to 2, affecting all the affluent equally, but still only the affluent. The Senate, where the strength of the Progressives was concentrated, voted to increase the surtax on high incomes to 13 percent and eliminate the exemption on dividend income, placing the increased tax burden entirely on the very rich. It also added a tax on estates of over $50,000, an amount that limited that tax as well to the affluent. The Senate's position prevailed.

This was social engineering pure and simple, for everyone agreed on the revenue needed. It was only a question of what parts of society, as measured by income, would pay it. Conservatives wanted lower rates on the wealthy in order to stimulate capital formation; liberals wanted high rates to allow tax relief for the poor and middle class. Conservatives, for reasons we will soon see, gave up the fight for a while. But ever since the Wilson era, it has been an accepted tenet of American liberalism that the

---

* As defined, of course, by intellectuals, since classes have no real-world analogue in this, the most socially fluid of nations. For generations, 90 percent of Americans have thought of themselves as middle class, when they thought about classes at all.

way to increase tax revenue is to increase marginal rates on the incomes of the rich. This worked at first in steeply raising revenues and in reducing the take-home income of the most affluent. But not for long.

In 1920, the last year of the Democratic dominance that had made the income tax possible, there were 5.5 million returns filed, about 13 percent of the labor force. But although only 1 percent of those returns were for incomes over $20,000, that group paid 70 percent of the income taxes. The rich, virtually untaxed as late as 1909, were, eleven years later, bearing the major burden of what had swiftly become a major provider of federal revenues, the income tax. Like the barons of thirteenth-century England who had forced the king to sign the Magna Carta when he tried to increase taxes, they didn't like it. And like the barons, they did something about it.

As David Houston, Wilson's last secretary of the treasury explained, "It seems idle to speculate in the abstract as to whether or not a progressive income tax schedule rising to rates in excess of seventy percent is justifiable. We are confronted with a condition, not a theory. The fact is that such rates cannot be successfully collected."

The reason, of course, was that the rich were quickly moving their assets in order to shelter their incomes, such as into state and local bonds that were tax exempt and into personal holding companies that were taxed at the much lower corporate rate.

In the election of 1920 the Republicans were swept back into power under the slogan of a return to "normalcy," and there was no question that normalcy included a return to the old order with regard to the level of taxes and dealing with the debt, now at $24 billion, not far from ten times its level at the end of the Civil War. Wartime taxes, as always, were fiercely opposed once peace returned. To oversee this return, the new president, Warren Harding, appointed banker Andrew Mellon to be secretary of the treasury.

Mellon had been born in Pittsburgh in 1855, where his Scotch-Irish grandparents had settled after immigrating from County Tyrone when his father, Thomas, was five. Thomas became a lawyer and was for ten years a judge in Allegheny County, before leaving the law to found a private bank, T. Mellon and Sons, in 1869.

The elder Mellon soon exhibited a gift for picking the right entrepreneurial horses to back with capital, including Andrew Carnegie and Henry Clay Frick. The latter quickly became close friends with Andrew Mellon, seven years his junior. Mellon would soon introduce Frick to the woman he was to marry, and Frick did the same for Mellon two decades later. In 1880 they took a trip to Europe together and both began to collect art, collections that would blossom over the course of their lives into two of the greatest private holdings in the world.*

If Thomas Mellon had a gift for spotting the up-and-coming entrepreneur, his son Andrew had a genius for it, a genius his father recognized, for he turned over the operation of the bank when the younger Mellon was only twenty-seven. The latter quickly began

---

* Frick would leave his collection to the city of New York, together with his Fifth Avenue mansion, where it is still housed, and a substantial endowment. Mellon gave his to the nation, building and endowing the National Gallery in Washington to hold it.

investing in companies—including the Carborundum Company and Gulf Oil—that would turn the Mellon fortune into one of the largest the country has known.

But Mellon's greatest investment was in a company built around a process invented by Charles M. Hall to extract aluminum from ore. Aluminum is one of the most abundant elements on earth, but it was little more than a chemical curiosity until Hall developed a means of using electricity, newly available in large amounts in the 1880s, to produce the pure metal in commercial quantities. He had little luck finding funding, however—since nothing was then made of aluminum, potential investors thought, who needs it? Finally he went to Andrew Mellon, who saw the possibilities in a light, ductile, nonrusting metal immediately. He invested heavily in the company that would grow into Alcoa.

Mellon was a man of moderate height, slat-thin, with pale blue-gray eyes and an ample mustache. He was also apparently a confirmed bachelor and devoted to business. But when he was forty-three, he fell in love with Nora McMullen, the beautiful, lively daughter of a very successful English brewer. She was less than half his age and at first reluctant to marry him, but he persisted and she finally accepted in 1900. The marriage would produce two children but was otherwise a disaster for they were basically incompatible, with little in common. He was quiet, a man who disliked parties and hated public speaking. She felt isolated in Pittsburgh and had no interest in his business dealings.

The marriage ended in divorce in 1912, and Mellon devoted himself more than ever to business and, increasingly if behind the scenes, to conservative Republican politics. So retiring was he, however, that when President-elect Harding nominated him for the Treasury post he was almost completely unknown to the public despite being one of the richest men in the country.

Mellon would prove to be the most influential treasury secretary since Alexander Hamilton, for the major problems facing the federal government in the 1920s—the national debt, taxes, and the economic consequences of World War I—all necessarily involved the Treasury. And Mellon, with his banker's ways and undoubted gift for handling with ease questions involving billions, seemed the perfect person to be secretary of the treasury in that business-minded decade. Also, of course, his aristocratic, retiring personality and complete personal integrity contrasted very favorably with many others who joined the Harding administration, one of the most corrupt in the nation's history. Mellon became so influential in Washington in fact that liberal senator George Norris joked that "three presidents served under Mellon" during his twelve years in office.

Mellon remained true to the old consensus that had guided American fiscal policy since Hamilton. He explained in *Taxation: The People's Business*, a book he wrote in 1924, that "since the war two guiding principles have dominated the financial policy of the Government. One is the balancing of the budget, and the other is the payment of the public debt. Both are in line with the fundamental policy of the government since its beginning."

Mellon set to work immediately on both sides of the fiscal equation, revenues and spending. The Republicans cut federal spending by 50 percent between 1920 and 1927, and would reduce the national debt as a result by one-third in the 1920s. As a percentage of GNP, they cut it by more than one-third.

But Mellon's greatest mark would be in taxes. Mellon believed unabashedly in what has only since the mid-1950s been called trickle-down economics. He thought that cutting taxes on the rich was the quickest means of building capital, lowering interest costs, and increasing investment. That, in turn, would ensure a prosperous, growing economy and thus higher revenues for the government and higher wages for workers. He quickly persuaded Congress, if not wholly to adopt his program, at least to move sharply in his direction.

Congress would lower tax rates three times in the early 1920s, until the top rate was down to 25 percent and many middle-class families were off the tax rolls altogether. This resulted in two surprising phenomena. The first was that revenue from the personal income tax did not fall. Indeed, it rose from $690 million in 1921 to $711 million five years later.

Even more curious, the distribution of the tax burden became radically *more* progressive, not less. In 1921 those earning less than $10,000 had paid $155 million in taxes, 21 percent of personal income tax revenues. In 1926 they paid only $33 million, or 5 percent. Mellon himself boasted in 1928 that a bachelor with a $4,000 income in 1920—enough to make him comfortably middle class—would have paid $120 in tax that year, but in 1928 would owe only $5.63.

At the same time the very rich, those earning over $100,000, saw their portion of income taxes rise from 29 percent to 51 percent, paying $194 million in 1921 and $362 million in 1926.

These results did not surprise Mellon. Indeed, *Taxation: The People's Business* explained them clearly, using reasoning that the economist Arthur Laffer would make famous all over again in the 1970s.

"It seems difficult for some to understand that high rates of taxation do not necessarily mean large revenue to the Government, and that more revenue may often be obtained by lower rates. There is an old saying that a railroad freight rate should be 'what the traffic will bear'; that is, the highest rate at which the largest quantity of freight would move. The same rule applies to all private businesses. . . . The Government . . . can and should be run on business principles."

That philosophy was widely accepted in the 1920s and worked well during that largely prosperous era. The debt, over $25 billion in 1919, was reduced to $16 billion by 1930. But when the economic situation began to change at the end of the decade and government fiscal and economic policies did not, the result was the greatest national crisis since the Civil War.

The Federal Reserve, which had been created in 1913, was largely leaderless in 1929. It had been increasingly dominated since its founding by Benjamin Strong, the governor of the New York Federal Reserve, and when he died in the autumn of 1928, no one replaced him as a maker of monetary policy.

Benjamin Strong, like so many who have deeply affected the country's fiscal and monetary affairs, came from old New England roots. Born in 1872, at eighteen he went to work for Jessup, Paton, and Company, private bankers in New York, and rose swiftly in New York's burgeoning financial market. It was soon clear that Strong was born to be a banker.

He married in 1895 and fathered four children, but he was not to know domestic happiness. His wife committed suicide in 1905, and Strong's neighbor Henry Davison, a partner of J. P. Morgan and Company, took Strong's children into his own household. Strong's second marriage was a failure, his wife leaving him in 1916, the same year he contracted tuberculosis.

Lonely and often sick, Strong threw himself more and more into his work, rising ever higher until he became president of the Bankers' Trust Company, then dominated by the Morgan interests. He would quite probably have soon achieved the pinnacle of American banking at that time, a Morgan partnership, had he not been persuaded to become governor of the newly created New York Federal Reserve.

Strong had at first refused the job because he did not approve of how the system was structured. While the panic of 1907 had finally convinced doubters that a central bank was indispensable to a modern industrial economy, the fear of the money trust (to use the turn-of-the-century term), so strong a feature of the Democratic Party since Jefferson's day, severely affected its design.

The great New York banks wanted a single central bank, modeled on the Bank of England and located in New York. After all, that was where the money was. Instead, the Federal Reserve as finally approved by Congress consisted of twelve independent banks, one in New York, the rest in cities all over the country. They were supposed to be coordinated by a board that sat in Washington, D.C., but Strong thought that the board would have political thumbs all over it, and wanted nothing to do with the Federal Reserve.

His mentor at J. P. Morgan and Company, Henry Davison, insisted, however, and Strong relented. He immediately set out to make the New York Federal Reserve in fact, if not in theory, the central bank of the United States. In large measure he succeeded.

He did so first of all because New York at that time utterly dominated American finance, while the outbreak of World War I made it indispensable to world finance as well (it soon replaced London as the world's most important money center).

Even more vital was Benjamin Strong's expertise and personality. He had been quite right that the Federal Reserve Board in Washington would consist largely of political appointees, many of them ignorant even of the basics of commercial banking, let alone the arcane world of central banking. But that meant they had no choice but to rely on Strong, who had a profound understanding of both. By the 1920s, despite the ever-worsening tuberculosis that was to kill him, Strong was the unquestioned boss of the Federal Reserve.

The age-old crosswinds of banking apply just as much to central banks as to ordinary ones, however, with the added problem of politics. The dislocations of the war still affected Europe, and Strong was anxious to help, realizing that American prosperity was at risk unless Europe was prosperous too. To do this, he had to keep American interest rates low so that European capital would stop flowing across the Atlantic and be put to use at home. But low interest rates fueled the already booming speculation on Wall Street. Strong had to balance the conflicting forces.

In 1927 Strong lowered the New York Federal Reserve discount rate (the rate at which member banks could borrow from the Fed) to 3.5 percent, from 4 percent. The other Federal Reserve banks followed suit. Herbert Hoover, then the secretary of commerce, was opposed to this move. Hoover considered Strong "a mental annex of Europe" and would go to his grave insisting that the Great Depression had its origin on that continent.

Certainly the lower interest rates stimulated Wall Street still further, but when speculation threatened to get out of hand, Strong acted to stop it. He raised the discount rate three times in 1928, up to 5 percent, a very high rate in those days, while he began a policy of increasingly restricting the money supply. "The problem now," Strong wrote, "is to shape our policy as to avoid a calamitous break in the stock market . . . and at the same time accomplish if possible" the recovery of Europe.

The new Fed policy had its effect on the real economy—the one beyond Wall Street—which slowed down noticeably in early 1929. This should have cooled down Wall Street as well. There, however, what had been a traditional bull rally turned into a classic bubble. The market lost contact with the underlying economy and predictions of an ever-rising market became, temporarily, a self-fulfilling prophecy. Immediate action by the Fed was needed, but, in a tragedy that reached far beyond the personal, Ben Strong had died the previous October, after one, last, desperate operation to stem his tuberculosis.

The now leaderless Federal Reserve did nothing. It kept the discount rate at 5 percent, where Strong had left it the summer before. Far worse, it allowed bankers to use the Fed itself to bankroll the increasingly reckless speculation.

In the spring of 1929 the interest rate for call money soared. In those days stocks could be bought with as little as 10 percent cash. Bankers could borrow at the Fed discount window, at 5 percent, and then lend the money, via the brokers, to speculators at 12 percent; billions moved to Wall Street this way. The Federal Reserve tried "moral suasion," asking the bankers to stop the practice.

Moral suasion is one thing, human nature quite another. If it is legal to earn 7 percent by using, in effect, someone else's money, people are going to do it. The bubble expanded until the "calamitous break" Strong had feared became inevitable.

And once the crash was over and the depression began to deepen, the Federal Reserve *still* did nothing, leaving the high interest rates of the late 1920s in place. Strong would have known what to do under the new circumstances, and there can be little doubt that he would have done it.

At the end of his life he wrote that "the very existence of the Federal Reserve System is a safeguard against anything like a calamity growing out of money rates . . . we have the power to deal with such an emergency instantly by flooding the Street with money" in order to abort a panic. Instead, the Fed stood by and watched the nation's money supply shrink by fully one-third over the next three years.*

The Fed's terrible mistake in monetary policy of continuing to treat the patient—the U.S. economy—for fever long after it had begun to freeze to death was compounded by two other profound mistakes in Hoover's fiscal policy.

The first was the Smoot-Hawley tariff passed in the spring of 1930 and signed by President Hoover to fulfill a campaign promise made in the different economic world of 1928. Its purpose was to protect the American market for American goods, and thus protect

---

* At least the Fed learned its lesson. As early as noon on October 19th, 1987, the day of the next great crash, the Fed was letting Wall Street leaders know that it was ready, willing, and able to help maintain liquidity in the market. This played no small part in ensuring that the crash of 1987 had few long-term consequences for the economy as a whole.

American jobs and profits. What resulted was a collapse of world trade—and thus American exports—as other countries followed suit with their own tariff walls, each adopting in turn a beggar-thy-neighbor policy. U.S. exports had been valued at $5.241 billion in 1929. In 1932 they were a mere $1.611 billion, the lowest they had been, allowing for inflation, since 1896.

But the Smoot-Hawley tariff, whatever its purpose, was also a tax. All tariffs are. Its domestic effect, therefore, was to decrease demand as foreign goods became more expensive and domestic competitors took advantage of that to raise their own prices.

The result, of course, was less, not more, tariff revenue and a quickly widening budget deficit. By 1931 the deficit was projected at $750 million just for the first quarter, an unprecedented sum for peacetime. The debt would stand at $16.8 billion by the fiscal year's end on July 1st. A year later it would be more than $19 billion. President Hoover was reluctant to raise taxes under the circumstances, but economists in those days were nearly unanimous in their recommendations to do so, and Hoover went along, still faithful to the idea that governments, like families, must balance their budgets.

It is ironic that one of Andrew Mellon's last acts as secretary of the treasury—he left office in early 1932 to become ambassador in London—was to ask Congress to undo most of his work in the 1920s. The top marginal rate moved back to 55 percent, where it had been in 1922.

The results of these further tax increases were utterly disastrous, slowing the economy still further. This, in turn, adversely impacted government revenues and increased the deficit markedly rather than reducing it. (The debt during the Hoover administration went from under $17 billion to more than $22 billion, higher than it had been at any time since 1922.) All of these factors also helped to ensure Hoover's overwhelming defeat in the 1932 election.

Together, these three political errors in judgment converted what had begun as an ordinary recession into the national calamity of the Great Depression. Among its casualties would be not only the blasted lives of millions of Americans and uncounted billions in lost wealth, but also the old pay-as-you-go consensus regarding the nation's proper fiscal policy.

Chapter 5

KEYNESIANISM AND THE
MADISON EFFECT

IN THE 139 years encompassing the period 1792–1930, the federal government ran a surplus ninety-three times and a deficit forty-six times, a two-to-one ratio. In the eighty years since 1930, however, it has had a surplus in only eight of them and a deficit in seventy-one, almost a one-to-nine ratio.*

What happened?

One answer, of course, at least for the first few years of the period, was the onset of the Great Depression. Not since the dark days of the early 1890s had the national economy caused massive budget deficits. As world trade collapsed, corporate profits vanished, and the incomes of those rich enough to pay income taxes steeply declined, government revenues plunged. Over $4 billion in 1930, they were less than $2 billion in both 1932 and 1933. Meanwhile, government outlays increased sharply as cries for federal relief funds became undeniable. Outlays were $3.3 billion in 1930, and $4.7 billion in 1932, an increase of more than one-third. The deficit that year amounted to 142 percent of revenues,

---

* In 1952, uniquely, spending exactly matched revenues.

by far the worst peacetime deficit* in the nation's history. Fortunately, because the securities of a sovereign power are the safest possible investment in bad times, the Treasury was able to borrow at very low interest rates. Indeed, so great was the fear of total financial collapse among the nation's remaining rich that the interest rate on Treasury bills—the federal securities with the shortest maturity—actually went negative in the fall of 1932. In other words, people were actually *paying* for the privilege of investing their money with the government.

But the Great Depression also scarred the country's psyche profoundly. It changed American attitudes toward economic priorities in much the same way as the German hyperinflation of the early 1920s—which wiped out the economic security of that country's middle class in a few harrowing months—made Germans acutely sensitive to the dangers of inflation. Since 1932, the first priority of federal economic policy has been to avoid, at all costs, another Great Depression. If that meant the abandonment of the old pay-as-you-go consensus on fiscal matters, so be it.

Elected at the bottom of the depression in November 1932, Franklin Roosevelt, like Hoover, had at first accepted the conventional wisdom regarding deficits. He largely based his presidential campaign that year on lambasting Hoover's fiscal mismanagement. "Let us have the courage to stop borrowing to meet continuing deficits," Roosevelt said in a radio address in July, echoing Adam Smith. "Revenues must cover expenditures by one means or another. Any government, like any family, can, for a year, spend a little

---

* 2009's deficit is estimated at 85.3 percent of revenues.

more than it earns. But you know and I know that a continuation of that habit means the poorhouse."

No sooner was he in office himself, however, than Roosevelt made an unbalanced budget a matter of deliberate policy for the first time in the history of the Republic. His advisers quickly convinced him that "passive deficits," which derive from falling tax receipts in bad times, not deliberate increases in spending, were, under the circumstances, good policy. They should be tolerated, the advisers thought, because any attempt to balance the budget would only make matters worse, as Hoover's taxes had. And everyone recognized that matters could not get much worse without threatening domestic stability itself.

In any event, Roosevelt—who possessed in spades the gut political instincts that Hoover the technocrat completely lacked—was not about to continue the policies that had destroyed Hoover's presidency, despite his campaign rhetoric. It is a measure of Roosevelt's greatness, as well as his philosophical flexibility, that he never let the hobgoblin of foolish consistency limit his policies.

While allowing passive deficits during the crisis, Roosevelt had no trouble discerning also that new spending programs were politically popular, whereas new taxes, as always in peacetime, most emphatically were not. Thus the extraordinary conditions of the 1930s allowed Roosevelt to institute an array of new federal programs, collectively known as the New Deal, mostly designed to provide jobs to the unemployed, which more than doubled federal spending between 1933 and 1940, from $4.6 billion to $9.6 billion. During that time there was little increase in military spending, so virtually all of the increased federal spending was for domestic programs.

But these new programs added "active deficits" to the passive ones caused by the depression, for Roosevelt moved very cautiously regarding taxes during the first two years of his presidency, mindful again of the fate of his predecessor. By 1935, however, confident in his popularity, he was moving sharply to the left and to the left's now traditional means of increasing government revenues, high and progressive marginal rates on large incomes. He condemned "economic royalists" and proposed what soon was dubbed "the wealth tax." It raised marginal rates on personal income back up to World War I levels and added a graduated corporate income tax up to 40.5 percent. It also increased estate taxes that impacted only the rich.

Because these new taxes affected only a very small segment of the population—the segment regularly kidded in Peter Arno cartoons of the period—Roosevelt paid hardly any political price for imposing them. But the amount of money they brought into the Treasury was disappointing, and the national debt continued its upward spiral begun in the Hoover years. Twenty-two billion dollars when Roosevelt took office, it was at $43 billion when prosperity fully returned in 1940 and military, not domestic, spending began to drive the budget.

The reason revenues did not rise as expected, of course, was that the rich reacted in an entirely predictable way—a way Andrew Mellon *had* predicted in 1924: They began to shelter income again. And by this time their lawyers, accountants, and lobbyists in Washington had mastered the art.

The result over the ensuing decades has been a classic example of what biologists call coevolution. Those faced with steeper and steeper income tax rates have developed ever newer and better ways to shelter income in the interstices of the conflicting tax laws. Meanwhile, Congess and the tax authorities have been trying to prevent or govern (and, pushed by lobbyists, not infrequently, to allow and even encourage) each new loophole. The result has been an unending explosion in the size of the tax code and the number of people lobbying for changes in it. Today, just the table of contents of the tax code is nearly 300 kilobytes long on the Internet* and the site warns that it takes a while to download. As of 2006, the number of pages in the tax code was 3,387. The *U.S. Code of Federal Regulations*, written by the IRS and, in effect, the Talmud to the Torah of the tax code, is twenty volumes long, totaling 13,458 pages. The number of registered lobbyists, many working on tax issues, was over 34,000 in 2005, according to the *Washington Post*. But many lobbyists are unregistered.

In the early days, some of the loopholes were lulus. Sailing as a guest on a Vanderbilt yacht one day, Roosevelt was astonished to learn that many rich men were incorporating their yachts in order to pay the expenses of running them out of pretax income and deduct the cost of "renting" them as a business expense. Setting up offshore corporations became popular. A New York financier was overheard in a Paris bar proudly proclaiming that "my fortune is in the Bahamas, and is going to stay there as long as that bastard is in the White House." He was by no means the only one to take similar action. The art of the expense account, an efficient means of providing tax-free income to employees, was quickly elaborated. Corporations would often provide luxurious

---

* http://www.irs.gov/taxpros/article/0,,id=98137,00.html.

apartments free of charge to their top executives in such desirable cities as New York, Paris, and London. In recent years the rich, or more properly their tax advisers, realized that a perfectly legitimate investment strategy called "selling against the box," which involves selling borrowed stock while continuing to hold the same stock, could also be used legally to avoid capital gains taxes when selling sharply appreciated assets. This strategy was outlawed in 1997.

And Congress, while retaining and even increasing very high marginal rates, began to write political favors into law. It created different categories of income and increased the number and kind of deductions. For instance, early in the Roosevelt administration there was an outcry that the rich were avoiding paying taxes by selling stocks at depressed prices—to establish capital losses they could use to offset regular incomes—and then buying back the stock to maintain control of the corporation.* Congress limited the deductibility of capital losses against regular income but at the same time sharply cut the tax rate on capital gains. This was no small matter when the stock market began to recover.

Congress also added an ever-increasing number of provisions that are nearly meaningless to the uninitiated (and almost impossible for the political reporters covering Congress for the mass media to explain to their readers and viewers), but which have had the effect of saving individual companies and even individual taxpayers millions in taxes.

---

*J. P. Morgan, Jr., spent much of 1934 cruising the world on his imperially scaled yacht *Corsair* but paid no income taxes at all that year, thanks to capital losses.

To give just one example, consider what Wall Street quickly dubbed "flower bonds," because they were usually bought shortly before a funeral. These were long-term treasury bonds that paid very low interest, which meant that they sold for much less than their face value. But they could be used, at their face value, to pay federal estate taxes, thus effectively lowering the real tax rate—as opposed to the nominal tax rate (the rate stated in the law)—on estates. The only problem was that flower bonds, which were not an attractive investment for those in good health, had to be in the estate at the time of death; they could not be purchased afterward by the estate. That's why Wall Street brokerage firms had a rule that orders for flower bonds were always to be executed immediately, to ensure that they were actually owned by the purchaser before he breathed his last.

Not all of these changes in the tax code benefited only the rich, however. In 1947 Congress exempted company-provided health insurance from income taxes. It was a well-intentioned act—not to mention extremely popular—that would do much to bring about the crisis in health care costs in future decades. Because increasing numbers of people no longer paid for their own health care, or even paid the premiums on the insurance that paid for it, they became ever more indifferent to the cost of health care. Freed of market restraints, health care costs began to spiral upward at a rate that exceeded both inflation and developing technology. When the federal government began funding a major portion of the country's health care with Medicare and Medicaid in the 1960s, the exploding costs of health care would play no small part in the explosion of the debt in the next two decades.

The end result of this inevitable process has been both the most complicated income tax code the world has ever seen and a great deal of income that goes entirely untaxed. Today it is estimated that the "tax gap" between taxes owed and taxes paid exceeds $300 billion. The process also made the tax code highly inflexible as an instrument of government policy, one unable to affect the revenue side of the fiscal equation in any predictable way. Roosevelt once described getting the bureaucracy to do something he wanted done as being "like punching a pillow." That is an excellent description of what it is now like to try to alter government revenues through the tax code.

The Roosevelt spending programs proved enduringly popular, even as better times began to return. So the increased tax revenues the improved economy brought were applied largely to extending the new social safety net, not to balancing the budget, still less to reducing the debt. Further, the percentage of the gross national product that passed through Washington began to climb sharply. Federal outlays amounted to 3.7 percent of GNP in 1930. By 1940 they were 9.1 percent. That percentage has been climbing more or less steadily ever since. In 2008 federal outlays amounted to about 17.6 percent of GDP. It is, perhaps, not going too far to say that Franklin Roosevelt and the Great Depression changed the country's perception of the proper scope of the federal government's responsibilities as much as Abraham Lincoln and the Civil War had changed the country's perception of itself.

It was the Second World War, however, not the New Deal programs, that finally ended the depression. And, needless to say, the war only increased the deficits. The worst of the war-years deficits occurred in 1943, when expenditures exceeded revenues by 214 percent. But that was far less, in percentage terms, than the worst deficits of World War I, which reached 260 percent, let alone those of the Civil War.

One reason the war's deficits were not higher was that for its duration the United States had in effect a centrally planned rather than a free-market economy, with such features as forced savings and fixed prices. Another was that the wartime prosperity—the unemployment rate was effectively zero—created much disposable income that could be taxed away by the income tax that now reached down deep into the middle class. Nonetheless, by 1946, the United States had run sixteen straight deficits, twice the previous record string, run up in the Civil War era. The national debt stood at $269 billion, 100 times what it had been at the end of the Civil War and almost 17 times what it had been in 1930. The war years alone added $211 billion to the national debt.

But now, for the first time after a great war, debt reduction was not the first object of federal fiscal policy, despite the return of both peace and prosperity. The most influential economist since Adam Smith, England's John Maynard Keynes (Lord Keynes after 1942), had changed the central concepts of economics profoundly. American fiscal policy would never be the same again not only because of the Great Depression but because Keynes supplied a philosophy to replace Adam Smith's imperative of balancing the budget whenever possible and paying down any debt as quickly as possible. Keynes was born in Cambridge, England, and he would be associated with Cambridge University and especially King's College for most of his life. He grew up to be ugly, bisexual (he would have a long affair with the biographer Lytton

Strachey before deciding to marry), and possessed of one of the finest minds of the twentieth century. A brilliant investor—by no means a common attribute among great economists—he would make a fortune for himself and greatly increase the endowment of Cambridge and King's College, where he studied and taught as well.

During the First World War Keynes worked for the British Treasury and went to the Versailles peace conference as one of its senior officials. But as the conference progressed, he found himself in increasing disagreement with his government over the imposition of a draconian peace. He felt that the economic burdens being placed on Germany were more than the German economy could bear and that the impact on the world economy would, inevitably, be severe.

He quit his post and wrote a book, *The Economic Consequences of the War*, that caused a sensation with its predictions of world economic dislocation and its attacks on both Prime Minister Lloyd George and President Wilson. Its predictions, of course, turned out to be all too true. With the onset of the Great Depression, he turned his formidable mind to its origins and its cure.

Before Keynes, economists had been largely concerned with what is now called microeconomics, the myriad allocation of resources that determine prices and affect markets. In effect, economics had been concerned with the trees. Keynes, however, looked at the forest, the macroeconomic phenomena of aggregate demand and supply.

Keynes argued, in one of his most famous aphorisms, that while these must indeed balance out in the long run, it was equally true that, in the long run, "we are all dead." In the short runs by which human beings measure things, aggregate supply and demand often do not balance, with pernicious results. If demand outstrips supply, inflation occurs. If, on the other hand, total demand is insufficient, depression results. And both inflation and depression have self-reinforcing effects as they influence the behavior of the basic units of any economic system, human beings.

Keynes further argued that government could and should take an active role in affecting both aggregate demand and supply. When inflation threatens, Keynes thought, government could dampen demand by reducing the money supply, raising taxes, reducing government spending, or some combination of the three. Opposite government action could deal with an economic slowdown. The result of these "active" deficits and surpluses, thought Keynes, would be a smoothly functioning economic system, permanently high employment, and low inflation.

Equally important, Keynes stood Adam Smith on his head with regard to debt. He argued that families and nations are different economic beasts altogether and that prudence for one could indeed be folly for the other. A family, Keynes argued, must necessarily borrow from someone else, but a nation can borrow from itself, the debits and credits canceling each other out, at least macroeconomically, just as a child can borrow from a parent without affecting the family's net worth. The national debt—an often necessary but always undesired evil in classical economics—Keynes argued, therefore doesn't really matter.

There is no doubt that Keynes's theory is a mighty work of a mighty intellect. He published his seminal book, *The General Theory of Employment, Interest, and Money,* in 1936, and it had an immense and immediate impact throughout the intellectual world. It is not hard to see why. Like Adam Smith and unlike all too many other economists, Keynes commanded the English language, not that his book is easy reading. Further, his theory appeared to solve, as classical theory could not, many puzzles regarding how the Great Depression had come about and why it lingered so tenaciously.

But as a prescription for handling the economy in the messy real world, rather than in the mathematically beautiful but artificial constructs of economic theory, Keynes's theory has proved to have at least three fatal flaws, recognized, alas, only in retrospect, as fatal flaws so often are. Keynes himself, of course, did not live to see his theory fully applied in the real world, for he died of heart disease in 1946.

The first flaw is that Keynes still viewed the economic universe as economists had always viewed it, as a machine. Economics became a discipline in the eighteenth century, when Sir Isaac Newton's *Principia Mathematica* was the model for all intellectual theories. As a result, economists from Adam Smith on have looked to the Newtonian clockwork universe, humming along in response to immutable laws, as their model for the economic universe they sought to comprehend.

At the end of the nineteenth century, an Englishman named Alfred Marshall, trained as a mathematician and physicist, created what Keynes—Marshall's pupil at Cambridge—approvingly called "a whole Copernican system, by which all the elements of the economic universe are kept in their places by mutual counterpoise and interaction."

Marshall's model of the economic universe was self-regulating and inherently stable. Keynes substituted one that required an engineer—government—for maximum efficiency. Keynes's model has dominated economic thinking ever since, despite the fact that, even enormously expanded and refined, it has proved inadequate at best and often quite useless in predicting events in the real world.

The reason is simple enough. An economy is not a machine that cycles endlessly. Instead, in a modern, industrial world of rapidly evolving technology, it is highly dynamic and nonlinear. A far better model for an economy than the clockwork universe of Newton is the ecosystem of modern biology, where every part influences and changes every other part. And ecosystems, of course, do not cycle; they evolve, often in inherently unpredictable ways. Their elements are never in exactly the same relative position twice.

The unspoken assumption of the economy-as-machine paradigm is that a given action with regard to taxes, spending, or monetary policy will have a given, and predictable, result, just as putting more pressure on the gas pedal always makes a car move faster, the additional speed proportional to the additional pressure. But the basic parts of an economy are often unpredictable and always self-interested human beings, not bits of metal mindlessly obeying the laws of physics.

So the cogs in the American economy—you, me, and 307 million other human beings—are quite capable of interacting in totally unexpected ways. For example, after the Treasury predicted that a proposed cut in the capital gains tax in 1978 would cost $20 billion in lost revenues, Congress made the cut anyway and it resulted in $20 billion in *increased* revenues as people rushed to take advantage of the new lower rates to unlock their investments.

As another example, a 1990 tax on luxury boats and airplanes, which was predicted to raise $16 million, raised $58,000 instead. People simply stopped buying boats and airplanes. So rather than raising revenue, the new tax caused 10,000 layoffs in those industries. To use the car analogy again: In this instance stepping on the gas pedal didn't make the car speed up; it made the oil pressure drop.

The second fatal flaw in the Keynesian system is that timely and reliable information on the state of the economy is essential for politicians to make correct policy decisions. But even in a world filled with number-crunching computers that Keynes never dreamed of, this is not to be had. Final figures of even so basic a statistic as GDP come out *three years* after the period they measure. A recession is officially recognized only after two successive quarters of economic contraction. In other words, a slowdown isn't even called a recession until it is at least nine months old. Preliminary economic data, to be sure, are available in a few weeks, but they are highly unreliable and frequently, and grossly, revised in the ensuing months and years. Further, they are subject to interpretation and "spin" by politicians and editorial writers with an agenda—which most of them, being human beings, have. And sometimes the statistics themselves, the means by which we perceive the economic universe, are unreliable. There is growing evidence that the Consumer Price Index, the most common measure of inflation, may well overstate the real inflation by as much as a full percentage point (in other words, when the CPI measures inflation at 4 percent per year, it might actually be only 3 percent, no small difference when wages, pensions, and Social Security benefits are adjusted according to the CPI figures). This, in turn, throws doubt on such other vital statistical measures as productivity and real wages.

So guiding a modern dynamic economy in the way Keynes envisioned is a bit like trying to fly an airplane on instruments when the instruments tell you at best only what the situation was an hour earlier, and may even be giving you completely false data. The consequences when the policy was actually tried in its entirety, beginning in the Johnson administration, proved to be unfortunate.

The third flaw in Keynes's theory lies in human nature itself, a powerful force in the real world that Keynes totally ignored. For the Keynesian system to function, it must be applied dispassionately. Taxes must be cut and spending increased in bad times. In good times, however, taxes must be increased and spending cut. That might work in the benevolent despotism of Platonic myth, but in a democracy it has proved to be politically impossible. Spending programs always and immediately create powerful political pressures to maintain and expand them, generated by those who are the direct beneficiaries, while opposition to them is diffused among the rest of the population who must pay for them. Meanwhile, tax increases are always politically unpopular, especially if they are designed to raise serious money from a broad segment of the population. The result, of course, has been an ever-increasing amount of deficit spending since 1930.

One problem is that human nature predisposes us to recognize depression easily and quickly, but prosperity, like happiness, is most easily seen in retrospect. The 1980s, for instance, are today remembered as a time of plenty in this country, a decade when the GNP rose by 35 percent in real terms and we added an economy the size of Germany's to the one we already had. But the newspapers of the day were filled with stories about farmers losing their land, the big-three auto companies being taken to the cleaners by the Japanese, the supposed American imperial overreach, and the first stock market crash in nearly sixty years.

In an economy as vast as that of the United States, recession is always going to be stalking one region of the country or one sector of the economy, even if the overall trend is upward. Living day to day, ordinary citizens, politicians, and economic reporters alike all have a natural tendency to concentrate on the trees that have problems, not the forest that is thriving.

The flaws in Keynes's theory, of course, were not apparent in the beginning, only the theory's promise of making a world without depression possible. Economists took to it immediately. Within a decade of the publication of *The General Theory*, it was the overwhelmingly dominant school of economic thought throughout the profession.

But there was a second reason that Keynes so quickly swept the field among economists. It might be called the Madison Effect, in honor of James Madison's famous dictum that "Men love Power." After all, until Keynes, politicians had not needed economists for help with running the country any more than they had needed astronomers. But Keynes made them indispensable, and economists quickly realized that. And the political power that Keynesianism has given economists has made them, understandably, reluctant to abandon it, despite its failures. Like socialism, the theoretical promise of Keynesianism is so bright that its failures have always been ascribed, among the believers, to poor execution or minor flaws, not to fundamentally faulty theory.

Politicians took a little longer to come around. Those of Harry Truman's and Dwight Eisenhower's generation, born in the last decades of the nineteenth century, had been raised in the classical tradition, and many had actually read Adam Smith, David Ricardo, and John Stuart Mill in their youth. By the 1930s, these men were middle-aged and relatively unreceptive to new ideas, especially fundamental ones regarding how the world works.

Also, the predictions by the Keynesians regarding the postwar American economy proved very wide of the mark. They foresaw renewed unemployment when wartime production shut down. But inflation turned out to be the major problem when wartime wage and price controls were lifted, and the pent-up demand of the war years could not be met quickly enough. And even Keynesians, using any number of different variations on the Keynesian economic model, gave contradictory advice. Truman joked that what he needed was a one-armed economist, because the ones he had were always saying "on the one hand . . . but on the other hand."

The politicians, however, were also fully aware of the sharply different political fates of Hoover and Roosevelt. Passive deficits, therefore, were no longer questioned in times of recession, nor are they likely to be again. And fully Keynesian notions began to creep in. In 1946 Congress passed the first Full Employment Act, committing government to a policy of actively seeking high employment in the national economy, something that would have been unthinkable only twenty years earlier. That same year the President's Council of Economic Advisors was created within the White House itself to offer the president options for dealing with the economy as a whole.

Still, between 1946 and 1960 there were seven years of deficit and seven of surplus, all but two of the deficits small ones. The fact that two of those years of surplus were during the Korean War demonstrates clearly that the idea of pay-as-you-go still had powerful political appeal at midcentury. As late as 1957, Eisenhower's secretary of the treasury, George Humphrey, dismissed Keynesianism, sniffing that "I do not think that you can spend yourself rich." Although the national debt did not shrink during the postwar years in actual dollars (in fact, it rose from $269 billion to $286 billion between 1946 and 1960), it shrank by nearly one-third when inflation's effect on the dollar is taken into account. And the economy in these years grew swiftly. So the national debt, which had been nearly 130 percent of GNP in 1946, probably its highest point in history, was less than 58 percent of GNP by 1960.

But if Keynesianism was largely an alien, or at least an uncongenial, concept to those who served under Truman and Eisenhower, it had a powerful appeal for the new generation of politicians who came to power with John F. Kennedy after his election in 1960. They had been educated during the Great Depression and its aftermath. Many had been taught to think economically in Keynesian terms (the first edition of Paul Samuelson's thoroughly Keynesian introductory college textbook, which has sold in the millions, came out in 1948). More, they brought a new generation of economists into government, men raised on Keynes and true believers in his theory.

And again the Madison Effect exerted a powerful tug. Until Keynes, the business cycle had been regarded as a force of nature, no more to be influenced than the tides, and thus not within a politician's venue. Now, however, there was an elegant theory that not only justified political manipulation of the economy as a whole but virtually commanded it for the good of the country. By enlarging the scope of legitimate political action, Keynesianism enlarged the power of politicians. By the end of the 1960s, even so basically conservative a politician as Richard Nixon was able to say, without fear of contradiction, "We are all Keynesians now."

Moreover, politicians have a natural inclination to spend in general, even if they disagree fiercely about what, specifically, to spend on. After all, spending earns them the gratitude and, they hope, the votes of the beneficiaries. Equally, they hate to tax and perhaps lose the votes of those who have to write bigger checks to the government. Under the old consensus, pleasing both halves of the body politic had been largely impossible, and politicians spent much of their time choosing between them and hoping they guessed right and so kept their jobs.

But Keynesianism now gave them a heaven-sent political justification for pursuing their self-interests in *both* high spending and low taxes. It is little wonder that they did so and have continued to do so since Keynesianism first came to real power. Constantly enlarging government spending to meet one more perceived need, they avoided higher taxes either by paying for the spending with the increased tax revenues of an expanding economy rather than paying down the debt, or by actually increasing the debt, despite the prosperous times. All this was done, in fact, in the cause of continuing and increasing prosperity.

As for the deficits, as Keynes argued, they didn't matter economically because the country was borrowing from itself. To deal with the issue politically, Kennedy's economic advisers, led by Professor Walter Heller of the University of Minnesota, devised a means of justifying current deficits, called the full-employment budget. This purported to show what the federal budget would have looked like had the economy been operating at optimum. This full-employment budget showed that the government would have been operating in surplus over the previous few years, and thus any deficit in the actual budget was justified as a stimulus to the economy to help it reach the Holy Grail of optimum.

There was a big problem with this reasoning, even accepting the economy-as-machine paradigm on which it was based. The perfectly efficient machine exists only in theory. Real-world machines—and real-world economies—will always be less than perfect. So the full-employment budget was nothing more than an economic cloud-castle built up out of numerous assumptions, most of which could easily be changed to make the numbers come out as needed.

It should, of course, be stressed that the economists who guided presidents in the 1960s and 1970s were not dishonest. They genuinely believed in the power of their discipline to improve the functioning of the American economy. But they had, nearly to a man, spent their pregovernment careers in academia, often involved with the highly abstruse mathematical models of modern economic theory. To use an old political cliché, few if any of them had ever met a payroll, just as Karl Marx never once in his life set foot in a factory.

Partly because of their policies, in the 1960s the debt grew by nearly one-third, to $371 billion.

While the political attitudes toward the debt underwent a gradual sea change beginning after the Second World War, the tax system remained largely unchanged. As early as the beginning of World War II, the federal tax code had been quickly spiraling into the incoherence it has been in ever since and which makes it so inflexible an instrument for changing the amount of revenue raised. Of the 208 pages in the Revenue Act of 1942 (fifteen times the length of the original 1913 income tax act), fully 162 dealt with closing, or defining, loopholes in earlier revenue acts. Seventy-eight percent of the act, in other words, dealt only with the fiscal and economic consequences of earlier tax legislation.

The rest of the act, passed a few months after the attack on Pearl Harbor, almost coincidentally converted the income tax into a truly mass tax for the first time, which it has been ever since. With the advent of total war, it sharply raised taxes on the middle class, where the bulk of the income is in this middle-class country. In the words of one tax historian, it spread the income tax "from the country club . . . district down to the railroad tracks and then over to the other side of the tracks."

After the war, rates were lowered on the smaller incomes, but very high marginal rates were retained on higher ones. By that time, high marginal rates were liberal dogma, but the rich no longer complained very loudly. Indeed, when a Republican president and a Republican Congress were elected in 1952, for the first time since 1928, no attempt was even made to lower rates. There was a reason: The rich and their advisers had learned not only how to live with them but to flourish under them. For reasons Mellon had explained thirty years earlier, the people with higher incomes were paying a smaller percentage of the total taxes under the status quo, thanks to a near infinity of provisos that lowered their effective tax rates (the percentage of total income actually taxed away), often to below those imposed on the wage-earning middle class.

For this reason the failed experiment of high marginal rates continued to be supported by the unlikely combination of the liberals and the rich, just as the failed experiment of prohibition was long supported by the preachers and the bootleggers. Politics, as they say, makes strange bedfellows.

One highly effective means for the rich to offset high marginal rates at that time was allowable deductions, for a deduction from taxable income is worth more the higher the marginal tax rate on one's income. For example, if a person has a $10,000 deduction and a 14 percent marginal tax rate, the deduction, by lowering his taxable income by $10,000, will lower his taxes by $1,400. But if a rich person in the 91 percent bracket has a $10,000 deduction, his tax bill will be lowered by fully $9,100.

Nowhere was the leverage inherent in this fact more obvious than in the complete deductibility of interest costs, regardless of the purpose to which the borrowed money was put. This had been in the original income tax law of 1913 and was not changed until Ronald Reagan's administration instituted reforms in the mid-1980s. In the 1950s when the top tax rate was 91 percent, what was nominally a 5 percent interest rate was, thanks to the deductibility of interest payments, a mere .45 percent interest rate for the wealthy, with Uncle Sam picking up the other 4.55 percentage points in lost tax revenue. Thus a $50,000 swimming pool, built with borrowed money and financed at 5 percent, would cost its owner only $225 a year in net interest costs. To put this another way, an income tax system featuring high marginal rates and numerous deductions is a welfare program for the rich and a very generous one at that.

High marginal rates also hurt the economy as a whole because they cause money to be invested in nonproductive assets. For instance, if someone in the 91 percent bracket buys $100,000 worth of a stock that pays a 10 percent dividend, he would take home only $900 in income from it, after paying $9,100 in taxes on the $10,000 in income. So investing the $100,000 in, say, a Rolls-Royce, costs him only $900 a year in foregone income.

It is economic lunacy in a capitalist economy to channel investment into swimming pools, yachts, Rolls-Royces, and Rembrandts, which are static capital, instead of income-producing assets such as stocks and bonds that enlarge the economy.

It was the Kennedy administration that finally began the long march away from the high marginal rates and multiple deductions that had characterized the income tax since Roosevelt's first term. John F. Kennedy, basically a very cautious politician, was not well educated in the new economics and at first resisted his Keynesian advisers' advice that the best way to "get the country moving again" was to cut tax rates even though the government was running a deficit.

But he understood the pernicious effects of high marginal rates and myriad deductions, perhaps because he was aware of the vast discrepancy between the theoretical tax rate on his father's enormous income and the percentage of that income that was actually taxed away. Being a Democrat, Kennedy had political cover to do something about it, although he soon coupled it with the economy-stimulating across-the-board tax cut pushed so hard by his advisers. In 1964 the top marginal rate was lowered to 70 percent, and many aspects of the tax law designed to offset those high rates were eliminated. Just as in the 1920s, tax revenues increased even in the first year of the new rates, while those in the highest bracket declared more taxable income and paid more taxes than they would have had to do under the old law.

By the time the Kennedy tax reforms were in place, however, Kennedy had been murdered and the far more activist Lyndon Johnson was president. Johnson was an unabashed believer in using the powers of government for the good of the country, and the promise of Keynesianism had a powerful appeal for him. There were a total of nine major changes in tax policy during his administration, all in the name of stimulating or restraining the economy, rather than in changing the amount of revenue raised or reforming the tax code. There is absolutely no evidence, however, that any of them had the effect intended. What they certainly did do was make it much harder, indeed impossible, for businesspeople to plan ahead, something the economists appear never to have taken into account in making their recommendations. The old failure to merge the corporate and personal income taxes, of course, only compounded this problem.

And although the prospering economy led to increased tax revenue, it did not lead to debt reduction. In fact, since Kennedy's inauguration, the U.S. government has run a budget surplus exactly five times, in 1969 when the by-then galloping inflation unexpectedly swelled government revenues, and in 1997–2000.* Thanks to the inflation, however, the national debt stayed nearly flat in constant dollars in the 1960s while increasing in nominal dollars by one-third.

That was a greater increase than in any previous decade that did not involve total war or a major depression. But because the 1960s were also a decade of strong economic growth, the debt as a percentage of GNP continued to decline, although at a much slower pace than in the late 1940s and 1950s. By 1970 the national debt was only 39.16 percent of GNP, compared with 57.75 percent a decade earlier. In fact, it was lower than it had been at any time since 1932.

Keynesians, of course, took credit for the strong economic growth in that decade and pointed to the falling ratio of debt to GNP as proof that debt didn't matter to a sovereign power. In their confidence, they talked about being able to "fine-tune" the American economy, to use the now-infamous expression coined by Kennedy economic adviser Walter Heller. Keynesian mechanics would tweak the carburetor here and change the air filter there. And the American economy would purr away at peak efficiency.

In fact the Keynesian economic model—or, more precisely, all of the Keynesian economic models, for they were many—was about to run off the road in the high-inflation, high-unemployment economy of the 1970s, an economy that in Keynesian theory was thought to be impossible in the first place.

---

* As we will see, these "surpluses" result only from changes in federal bookkeeping instituted by the Johnson administration in 1968.

Meanwhile, political events and new political conditions were beginning to interact in Washington, and the budget of the U.S. government, the largest fiscal entity on the face of the earth, was about to spin out of control.

The national debt, in consequence, was about to explode.

Chapter 6

THE DEBT EXPLODES

THE FOUNDING FATHERS quite deliberately established a built-in power balance between the president and Congress. They gave to Congress those decisions, such as how much spending to allow, that reflect the diverse interests of the people. Equally they gave the president the powers that are best exercised by a single individual rather than a committee, such as command of the military.

But over the years since Washington took the oath of office, power has flowed back and forth between the White House and Capitol Hill several times. In great crises, when a strong—and unified—hand at the tiller was obviously needed, presidents like Abraham Lincoln and Franklin Roosevelt were able to get pretty much what they wanted from Congress. So too could presidents of extraordinary personality or surpassing political skills, such as Theodore Roosevelt and Lyndon Johnson. But when times were good or the White House was occupied by a weak president, such as Ulysses S. Grant or George H. W. Bush, Congress has tended to steadily encroach on the president's freedom of action.

Nowhere have the power shifts between president and Congress been more noticeable in the twentieth century than in regard to power over the budget. Remarkably, it was only in the aftermath of World War I, under Secretary of the Treasury Andrew Mellon, that the federal government for the first time began to develop an actual budget to facilitate looking at the whole picture, not just the sum of all congressional appropriations. Until 1921, each executive department had simply forwarded its spending requests to the secretary of the treasury, who passed them on in turn to the appropriate committee in the House.*

After the Civil War, both houses of Congress established appropriations committees to handle spending bills. Members who were not on these committees, however, envied an important power of those who were: that of dispensing money—then as now and always the mother's milk of politics—to favored groups. By the mid-1880s, eight of the fourteen annual appropriations bills had been dispersed to other committees. The former chairman of the House Appropriations Committee, Samuel Randall, predicted the then-far future accurately. "If you undertake to divide all these appropriations and have many committees where there should be but one," he wrote in 1884, "you will enter upon a path of extravagance you cannot foresee . . . until we find the Treasury of the country bankrupt."

By 1918 some departments had appropriations that were decided on by two or more committees, often working at cross-purposes. Many in Congress were disgusted with how such

---

* The Constitution mandates that all revenue bills originate in the House. By convention, spending bills originate there as well, giving the House the dominant congressional say in fiscal affairs.

important matters were handled. "The President is asking our businessmen to economize and become more efficient," Representative Alvan T. Fuller declared in 1918, "while we continue to be the most inefficient and expensive barnacle that ever attached itself to the ship of state."

In 1920 the House, by a bare majority, restored exclusive authority on spending bills to its Appropriations Committee, and the Senate followed suit two years later. But the House Appropriations Committee was considerably enlarged and split into numerous subcommittees that dealt with the separate spending bills. The committee as a whole usually had no practical choice but to go along with the subcommittee decisions. Power over individual appropriations, therefore, remained widely dispersed within Congress, while the ability to control and even determine total spending remained weak.

Soon after, in 1921, Congress passed the Budget and Accounting Act. This was intended to deal with the sudden upsurge in permanent federal spending brought on by the war. In 1916 the federal government had spent only 1.48 percent of GNP. Five years later, even with the immediate expenses of the war over, it was spending 7.27 percent, although that percentage would decline steadily throughout the 1920s. The act established the Bureau of the Budget, an arm of the Treasury Department, and the General Accounting Office,* an arm of Congress that was empowered to audit the various executive departments and to make recommendations for doing things cheaper and better.

---

* Its name was changed to the General Accountability Office in 2004 to reflect the fact that it performs not just financial audits but also performance audits.

The executive departments now had to submit their spending requests to the Bureau of the Budget, which put together revenue estimates and a comprehensive federal spending plan before the requests were transmitted to Congress. By establishing the Bureau of the Budget, Congress recognized the right of the president, as chief executive, to propose an overall spending plan, a traditional executive function. But because Congress then lacked the bureaucratic machinery, it had no choice but to accept the president's revenue estimates and could do little more than tinker with the president's spending proposals.

In 1939 Roosevelt, to tighten his grip on the budget even further, moved the bureau into the White House itself, where it was under his immediate thumb. (In 1970 it became the Office of Management and Budget, with expanded powers, but the legislation establishing the OMB required that its director and assistant director be subject to Senate confirmation.)

In 1946 Congress, wanting to increase its own power over the overall budget, passed the Legislative Reorganization Act. This required Congress to decide on a maximum amount to be appropriated each year before the actual appropriations bills were taken up. It was a dismal failure. In 1947 the Senate and House failed to agree on a maximum spending limit. In 1948 Congress simply disregarded the limit and appropriated $6 billion more than the spending resolution had called for, a better than 15 percent increase over the supposed limit. In 1949 it again failed to produce a resolution.

And Congress has often acted in ways that actually limited its ability to affect the budget as a whole. For instance, it steadily increased the amount of so-called backdoor spending—spending authorized in permanent legislation rather than in the annual appropriations bills—that had begun in the 1840s when Congress authorized the Treasury to pay the interest and principal due on the national debt without a specific appropriation. The members of the legislative committees in both houses still resented the power that the members of the appropriations committees and their subcommittees had over spending. By writing more and more spending into permanent law, such as the Aid to Families with Dependent Children program in 1935, the beginning of federal involvement in welfare, any changes in spending levels in the programs affected would have to pass through the committees that originated those laws in the first place.

The backdoor spending that has had the greatest destabilizing effect on the budget has been the "entitlements"—monies paid without limit to all who qualify in such programs as Social Security, Medicare, and Medicaid. Because these spending programs directly benefit many millions, the political forces behind their continuation and enlargement quickly became awesome. Soon they were being called the "third rail of American politics": Touch them and you die. Today, backdoor spending has grown to the point that it constitutes fully three-quarters of the entire budget but receives no direct congressional control whatever.

Congress's failure to set total spending limits in the 1940s under the Legislative Reorganization Act left the president still largely in control of the budget for the next two decades, thanks to his ability to forecast revenues and shape the overall budget and, increasingly toward the end of the period, his power of "impoundment."

In the Constitution, the Founding Fathers gave Congress an

explicit, but negative, power over spending: "No Money shall be drawn from the Treasury, but in Consequence of Appropriations made by Law." The Constitution is completely silent, however, on whether the president, in turn, is required to spend all the money that Congress appropriates. As noted, the Founding Fathers had assumed that the legislative branch would always be reluctant to spend whereas the executive would always be eager to. But as early as 1803, Thomas Jefferson (a passionate believer in a small federal government) informed Congress that he had not spent $50,000 it had appropriated for gunboats because of "the peaceful turn of events." Most presidents, up to Richard Nixon, did likewise from time to time.

In 1950 Congress even indirectly acknowledged a limited impoundment power by authorizing the president to take advantage of savings that were made possible by developments that occurred after an appropriation was made. But as Keynesianism became more and more entrenched and the old pay-as-you-go consensus began to wane, presidents were forced to use the impoundment power more often and more aggressively in order to keep total spending in check.

In 1966 Lyndon Johnson used impoundment to cut a very substantial $5.3-billion chunk out of a $134-billion budget. His aim was to damp down the inflation that the buildup of the Vietnam War was causing. The money impounded included $1.1 billion in highway funds and $760 million in such popular spending programs as agriculture, housing, and education. The Democratic-controlled Congress, needless to say, was not happy about this. But since Johnson was both a Democratic president and perhaps the greatest political arm twister in the country's history, he was able to get his way. In the following two years he impounded even larger sums, attempting to maintain control over a budget that in 1968 had a deficit equal to 16 percent of revenues, tying a postwar record set in the recession of 1958–59.

His successor, Richard Nixon, did not fare so well in his use of impoundment. Nixon, as he said, was a Keynesian. But as a Keynesian he knew that in times of high inflation and low unemployment, such as he faced when he entered office, it was time to tighten, not increase, federal spending. Mostly by coincidence, in 1969, Nixon's first year in the White House, the budget that was largely the work of the outgoing Johnson administration produced what would be the last surplus for twenty-eight years. Even that surplus amounted to only 2 percent of revenues.

Thereafter, congressional appropriations, despite the good times, continued to rise, and Nixon impounded more and more money. During the election of 1972 he called for a $250 billion spending ceiling for the following fiscal year, but the Senate rejected the request in October. Winning forty-nine states the following month, the reelected president decided to keep federal spending under that limit anyway, using the explicit power of the presidential veto and the implicit one of impoundment.

But Nixon, characteristically perhaps, went too far. Previous presidents had simply refused to spend money that Congress had appropriated. But in 1972 Congress passed the Federal Water Pollution Act, which Nixon vetoed as too expensive. When Congress overrode the president's veto, however, Nixon then impounded the $6 billion that the act appropriated.

This was a different matter altogether. Previous impoundments had often served Congress's purposes as well as the president's.

They allowed members to attach constituent-pleasing but expensive measures to bills and get them passed into law while the president then took any political heat for refusing to spend the money. But by refusing to spend the money appropriated over his veto, Nixon was, in effect, directly challenging Congress's constitutional authority to enact the laws, the very heart and soul of congressional power.

Hardly surprisingly, Congress reacted angrily. The Senate convened hearings on impoundment, chaired by Senator Sam Ervin of North Carolina, who would soon become a household name as chairman of the Watergate hearings. Ervin was the Senate's leading authority on the Constitution, and he thought that impoundment was flatly unconstitutional, being, in effect, a line-item veto.* Both the House and the Senate produced bills that would have severely restricted or even eliminated the president's impoundment authority. But no impoundment bill cleared Congress that session, and Washington was soon consumed with the unfolding Watergate scandal. The debt received little political attention during this period, despite the fact that the deficit in the fiscal year in which Nixon resigned reached $53 billion, the most, in dollar terms, since the middle of World War II.

As Nixon's political leverage began to erode swiftly, Congress set out to make itself dominant in the budget process, at the expense of the presidency. The result was what turned out to be the wildly

---

* The Supreme Court, as a matter of fact, has never ruled directly on the subject of impoundment, although lower courts have ruled against the president on the issue.

misnamed Budget Control Act of 1974. Nixon signed it on July 12th, not because he thought it was a good idea but because he knew any veto was futile. Less than a month later, developments in the Watergate scandal left him no viable political option but resignation. As Nixon left the White House in disgrace, the presidency was weaker, relative to Congress, than it had been at any time in the forty-one years since Franklin Roosevelt had been inaugurated.

The new Budget Control Act created the Congressional Budget Office, which gave Congress much the same expertise as the president enjoyed from the Office of Management and Budget and, of course, duplicated most of its work. Many subsequent budget disagreements between the White House and Capitol Hill have turned on whether to accept OMB or CBO figures and predictions, rather than on actual spending or taxing issues. Further, the act specifically forbade impoundment, substituting two new mechanisms, rescission and deferral. The first allowed the president to request Congress to remove particular spending items from appropriations, but unless both houses agreed the money had to be spent. Rescission has proved utterly useless as a means of budgetary discipline. The second mechanism, called deferral, was quickly ruled unconstitutional. With the Congress now possessing a budget bureaucracy of its own and the executive stripped of the power of impoundment, the president's only real remaining power over the budget was the veto of one or more of the fourteen appropriations bills, a sledgehammer at best. And, of course, the president had no power over the backdoor spending that now dominated federal spending and which did not even cross his desk.

But with the presidency already severely weakened by the folly of its most recent occupant, Congress, in writing the Budget Control Act, was much more concerned with the distribution of power within Congress itself. The original proposal of the joint committee that had been recently set up to review budget procedures had called for budget ceilings to be established early in the year. These ceilings, of course, would have greatly restricted the ability of Congress to begin new programs or enlarge old ones without raising taxes or taking the money from somewhere else in the budget. That, in turn, would have meant goring some other congressman's ox. Flexible "targets" were quickly substituted for rigid ceilings.

The reason, in this case, is simple. Congress as a whole has an interest in budgetary discipline, indeed it has a profound constitutional duty to impose budgetary discipline. But each individual member, at least those who want to make a career in Congress, has a profound self-interest in bringing home the bacon to his or her political constituency. With rare exceptions, the iron reality of the need to get reelected will always take priority over a relative abstraction like the budget deficit.*

As a result of the Budget Control Act, there was now little ability left, either in the Congress or in the presidency, to retard the modern Congress's natural inclination to spend. Further, a revolution in the House of Representatives that resulted in the overthrow of the seniority system removed virtually the last check on spending.

---

* This is a powerful argument for term limits, by the way, but one that, curiously, is seldom mentioned.

Under the seniority system, the senior member of a committee or subcommittee in the majority party was automatically chairman of that committee. This system had come into use in the early days of the century as a check on the once-unbridled power of the Speaker to name committee chairmen. But the large number of freshman representatives who entered the House in 1975, in the wake of the Watergate scandal (the Democrats gained no fewer than forty-five seats in the 1974 election), were, on average, young, liberal, and determined not to have to wait years to achieve real power in the House.

They forced a change in the rules so that the majority party caucus (all the members of that party meeting together) elected the committee chairmen at the beginning of each new Congress. In practice, this meant the Democratic caucus, for the Democratic Party had had a majority in the House for two decades and would continue to have one for two decades more.

In theory, this made the House much more "democratic." In reality, it made it nearly ungovernable. Under the seniority system, the committee chairmen, safe both in their seats and in their chairmanships, could look at the larger picture—the national interest—as well as their own political interests, and impose limits on the spending under their control. Under the new system, however, they had to secure the support of a majority of the caucus every two years to keep their chairmanships. That, of course, meant they had to make promises, and promises, in Congress, almost invariably mean spending money.

Another result of the Watergate scandal was campaign finance reform that put a ceiling of $1,000 on the amount that an individual could give to a political campaign.* The Supreme Court quickly threw out the limit with regard to people giving money to their own campaigns, on free-speech grounds, but, curiously, accepted it with regard to funding other campaigns. Using money to say "Vote for me," according to the Court, is protected by the First Amendment; using money to say "Vote for him" is not. Campaign costs, of course, did not go down, and this caused a search for new means of funding. The result was the Political Action Committee, or PAC system, which quickly blossomed and came to dominate political funding within a few years. The PAC system for funding campaigns, however, made the members of Congress less and less dependent on their home base and grass-roots support, and ever more dependent on the PACs. And behind every PAC is a spending constituency, urging the Congress to appropriate money.

The result of all this was an explosion of deficit spending because, almost literally, there was no one in Washington with the power or the inclination to stop it. The national debt nearly tripled in the 1970s, from $371 billion to $909 billion. Even adjusted for the galloping inflation of that decade, it rose more than 12 percent. And while, as a percentage of GNP, it had been falling swiftly every year since the end of the Second World War, in the 1970s it shrank only modestly, from 39 percent to 34 percent.

In fact, the only thing that kept federal deficits from getting a great deal worse than they did was the very high inflation the nation experienced during the 1970s. At one point in this pe-

---

* The amount was raised to $2,000 in 2002 and indexed for inflation. The limit for the 2010 election is $2,400.

riod, inflation reached an annual rate of 18 percent, higher than it had been even in the Civil War era when the government was paying a significant portion of its expenses with printing-press money.

Inflation causes assets with a fixed dollar value, such as federal bonds, to shrink in value relative to other commodities that can rise in price. This, in turn, causes the federal debt to shrink relative to the GDP, impoverishing the bond holders in the process. But inflation also causes nominal wages to rise sharply, while real wages rise much less, if at all. The ever-higher nominal wages that resulted from the inflation of the 1970s, however, pushed millions of people into higher and higher tax brackets, offering what would seem to be a politician's dream come true: a mammoth and continuing tax increase on real wages that didn't have to be voted on.

The Democratic Party, which had been the party of ideas in American politics since the era of the New Deal, and had set the agenda even during the occasional periods of Republican occupation of the White House, was deeply committed to social-welfare policies and was increasingly influenced by public-service workers' unions. It tended to see this increased tax revenue merely as an opportunity to enlarge government programs and to extend the so-called safety net.

The Republican Party, however, largely intellectually dormant since the Progressive era, began to bubble with new ideas in the 1970s. Many Republicans saw opportunity in the fact that the high marginal tax rates that were designed to place much of the tax burden on the rich—or perhaps more accurately, *appear* to do so—now reached down well into the middle class and even into the blue-collar voters who had long been the heart of the Democratic constituency. These people, whose incomes come overwhelmingly from wages, lacked the myriad loopholes that tax specialists had developed and that Congress had often enshrined into law for the benefit of the very rich.

No one saw this opportunity more clearly than a young congressman from Buffalo, New York, named Jack Kemp. He was among the first of a new breed of politician in this country, one who built a political career on the fame he earned in an entirely different profession (other than the military, of course). Born in 1935 in depression-racked Los Angeles, he grew up there and went to Fairfax High School, where he received, in his words, "an education by osmosis," because he spent as much time as possible playing football. He went to Occidental College in Los Angeles, a small school with a good football team because, as Kemp explained, "I wasn't big enough to go to USC or UCLA." But he knew what he wanted to do: "I was going to play football. I was going to play *pro* football."

And play pro football he did, for he made up in the riflelike accuracy of his throwing arm what he lacked in size. In his first year with the Los Angeles Chargers (the team became the San Diego Chargers the following year), he led the brand-new American Football League in passing, with twenty touchdowns. In 1962 he injured a finger, and the team put him on waivers in order to add another player to the roster until he was healed. But the Buffalo Bills unexpectedly snapped up his contract, and it would be in Buffalo over the rest of the decade that he would earn his lasting fame as a quarterback. By the time he retired, he had led the team to three division championships and two league championships.

By then he held the league records for passing attempts, completions, and yards gained in passing.

While playing football, Kemp was also getting a thorough (and this time nonosmotic) education in politics and economics. He had worked as a volunteer in Nelson Rockefeller's campaign for governor of New York in 1958 and in Nixon's 1960 presidential race. He took courses in education and political science and began reading economic history, which he described as "a road-to-Damascus-like experience." After Ronald Reagan was elected governor of California, he made Kemp an assistant to his chief of staff during the off-seasons.

So when Kemp, after his football career ended, was offered the Republican nomination for a congressional seat in suburban Buffalo, he was prepared. His opponent denounced his inexperience and his ties to Nixon, but Kemp, helped in no small way by his fame as a football hero, offered a program of "peace without surrender, prosperity without inflation, and justice without disorder." He narrowly won his first election but vastly increased his vote percentage in subsequent campaigns. In 1978 the Democrats did not even bother to field a candidate against him.

While he took relatively standard Republican positions on such matters as foreign affairs, he made a name for himself in espousing both deregulation and what has come to be known as "supply-side economics." The core premise of Kemp's and other "neoconservative" thinkers' philosophy is that human beings respond to incentives and that these can often be used far more efficiently than government regulation and government spending to move the country in a positive way.

As Kemp explained, "If you tax something, you get less of it. If you subsidize something, you get more of it. In America we tax work, growth, investment, employment, savings, and productivity. We subsidize nonworking, consumption, welfare, and debt."

In 1978 Kemp and Senator William Roth of Delaware proposed slashing tax rates for individuals by an average of 33 percent while, once again, plugging loopholes to broaden the tax base. The Democrats derided the proposal. House Majority Leader Jim Wright (himself later forced to resign as Speaker of the House in a financial scandal) called Kemp's idea "blatant hucksterism." Representative Otis Pike, Democrat of New York, thought that it should not be "voted down" but "laughed down." It failed to pass the heavily Democratic Congress, and when the Republican candidate for president in 1980, Ronald Reagan, embraced it, President Jimmy Carter started calling it the "Reagan-Kemp-Roth" tax proposal, hoping to tar his opponent with the brush of "tax cuts for the rich."

Jimmy Carter had many political burdens going into the election of 1980, but there is no doubt that the rapidly rising personal income taxes of people no one would call rich was a significant reason that he became the first elected president to be defeated for reelection since Herbert Hoover. Further, the Senate went Republican in the election for the first time in twenty-eight years.

At President Reagan's urging, Congress cut income taxes the first year he was in office, lowering rates to a high of 50 percent and once again slashing deductions. As before, once the tax cuts took full effect, in 1983, the government's total income tax receipts began to rise the following year, and the percentage of total taxes paid by those in the higher income range sharply increased.

In 1986, working with Democratic representative Dan

Rostenkowski, chairman of the tax-writing House Ways and Means Committee, Reagan was able to persuade Congress to slash rates again, this time to only two brackets, 15 and 28 percent, while eliminating most remaining open-ended deductions, such as the unlimited deductibility of interest payments. It was the greatest reform of the federal tax system since the introduction of the income tax itself and, as always, produced higher revenues and higher tax payments by the rich. In 1981 those with the top 1 percent of incomes paid 17.9 percent of total personal income taxes. In 1990 they paid 25.6 percent, a percentage increase of 43 percent. Meanwhile, federal tax revenues doubled in the 1980s and increased by more than 24 percent when adjusted for inflation.

Whereas Reagan was able to push through both tax reductions and wide-ranging tax reform—indexing tax brackets to inflation, for instance, so that they rose with inflation and no longer caused automatic tax increases—he was able to achieve real spending limitations only in the first year of his presidency. Thereafter, his budgets were declared "dead on arrival" as soon as they reached Capitol Hill.

Congress, however, was utterly unable to provide a coherent substitute. Indeed, more than once Congress couldn't pass a single appropriations bill before the start of the fiscal year, October 1st. It had to pass so-called continuing resolutions that allow federal departments to continue spending at current levels to avoid shutting down the government.

Most of the spending increases during Reagan's administrations came in the entitlements, such as Social Security, Medicare, and Medicaid, that were written into permanent law and thus did not cross the president's desk.

For his part, President Reagan was also determined to fund the Star Wars project he initiated and to continue the buildup of the military that had begun in the Carter years. He was able to push these expensive programs through Congress, and, after forty years, they finally helped bring victory in the Cold War. But Congress was unwilling to cut spending elsewhere to pay for them.

So federal spending continued to spiral upward with no relation whatever to revenues. The result, coupled with the $481-billion bailout required by the savings-and-loan debacle, was an avalanche of deficits. In the 1980s the national debt more than tripled, even more than it had in the 1970s, rising from $909 billion in 1980 to $3.2 trillion in 1990. But this time, inflation did not cushion the blow nearly so much, and the debt more than doubled in real terms. As a percentage of GNP, the national debt increased from 34 percent to 58 percent, the highest it had been in three decades. In the single year 1983 the deficit reached an awesome $208 billion, a sum greater than the entire federal budget as recently as 1970.

The apparent deficits, however, would have been far worse had it not been for a sharp increase in Social Security taxes in 1983 to fund future Social Security liabilities. Social Security is funded by a flat 15.30 percent tax on payrolls that is divided evenly between the workers and the employers. But this tax is highly regressive because while the tax is charged on the first dollar of income, it is not charged on any portion of wage income that is over $106,800 a year in 2009, whereas investment income is not taxed at all for Social Security. Thus a person paid $50,000 a year has 7.65 percent of that sum deducted from his paycheck for Social Security, but a person earning $1 million pays less than .5 percent.

Social Security taxes are, by law, deposited into the Social Security Trust Fund, out of which is paid Social Security benefits. Any surplus is invested in special Treasury-issued securities that pay an interest rate equal to an average of federal securities with maturities of more than four years. Until 1968, the Social Security Administration was "off budget." But Lyndon Johnson, anxious to make the apparent budget deficit that year look better than it was (it was, by far, the worst since the end of the Second World War), moved it "on budget." By being on budget the transfer of the Social Security surplus to the Treasury in exchange for federal bonds became merely a "transfer between government accounts." Thus the federal government could count the Social Security surplus as "income." This is sheer book cooking on a massive scale. To see how, imagine a company with a big loss for a year transferring employee contributions to the company pension fund to its own accounts, replacing the funds with newly issued corporate bonds, and calling the inflow of cash income. Corporate managers have gone to jail for less than that, but it is perfectly legal for the federal government to do so as the federal government decides its own accounting rules.

The Social Security surplus will soon disappear with the retirement of more and more baby boomers, those born between 1946 and 1964. It is currently projected to end in 2017, only seven years away. After that, the Treasury is not going to have a flow of surplus cash from the Trust Fund, but instead an ever larger amount of federal bonds being presented for redemption. To redeem those bonds, Congress will have three choices: raise taxes, cut spending, or issue other bonds to be sold in the public bond market. The slightly more than $2 trillion now in the Social Security Trust Fund will be exhausted in 2042, assuming normal economic growth over the next thirty years.

Numerous "summits" and "budget deals" between the president and Congress were held and numerous "budget reforms" were agreed to in the 1980s and 1990s. But none of them addressed the root cause of the problem: There was constant and intense political pressure to spend on specific programs, but no institutional check on total spending. Indeed 1985 was the first year the budget deficit became a major political issue, and the first of the laws meant to bring spending under control, known as Gramm-Rudman, was enacted. But that year Congress also initiated no fewer than fifty-four *new* benefit programs, bringing the total number of such programs to no less than 1,013.

Stripped of rhetoric, these attempts to rein in spending amounted to little more than business as usual today with spending cuts promised for tomorrow. None of them produced any lasting reversal of the trend to higher and higher deficits for the simple reason that the government was no longer institutionally capable of reversing it. In the first three years of the 1990s, the debt-to-GNP ratio rose another 10 percentage points, to over 68 percent, and in 1995 the debt topped $5 trillion.

Unable to cut spending, the government increasingly sought salvation on the tax side. In 1990 President George Bush, faced with an imminent war in the Persian Gulf, caved in to the Democratic majorities in Congress and broke his fundamental election pledge of "no new taxes." In 1992, with the people clearly unhappy with how the country's affairs were being handled, Democrat Bill Clinton ran for president on a platform of "fundamental change." A minority of a deeply divided electorate chose him and this platform, rejecting an elected president for only the second time since Hoover lost to Roosevelt sixty years earlier. And they gave Ross Perot, a third-party candidate who had never held elective office, a higher percentage of the vote than any third-party candidate had won since former president Theodore Roosevelt ran as a Progressive in 1912.

But an ossified congressional majority, while giving lip service to the Clinton agenda, in fact resisted any change in the status quo of how Congress worked, because they perceived it would have meant a change in their power. The Madison Effect held them in its grip. The very day after the 1992 election, the congressional leadership flew to Little Rock and advised President-elect Clinton to downplay the congressional and structural reforms that had been a major part of his program, in order to get the rest enacted.

Clinton, in a major political misjudgment, went along with the leadership. His frequent call for a line-item veto during the campaign was heard no more. His promises to change the way Washington worked were, in the words of Democratic senator Daniel Patrick Moynihan, "thrown out the window." It was to be business as usual for two more years.

But only for two years, as it turned out. Still another "budget deal" with Congress to curb the federal government's spending addiction was worked out in 1993, but it was a near carbon copy of the 1990 budget deal agreed to by President Bush that had done nothing to stem the annual deficits. President Clinton sought to raise marginal tax rates, and five tax brackets were created where only two had existed seven years earlier. This time, the Republicans would have none of it, and the budget passed with no GOP votes whatever. It carried in the House by a single vote only when several Democratic legislators were promised virtually anything if they would go along. It carried in the Senate only when the vice president broke a tie vote.

To be sure, the size of the annual deficit in dollar terms and as a percentage of revenue declined after this deal, but it was a matter far more of coincidence than causation. More important, as a percentage of GDP the national debt has continued to grow. One major reason for the decline of the deficit was the expansion the economy experienced after the recession of 1990 ended in early 1992, for federal deficits usually decline as the economy expands. Another major reason was the increase in revenues resulting from the sale of assets that had been taken over from failed savings and loan associations. The people reacted unequivocally at the next opportunity. In the 1994 midterm congressional election, they were given a clear choice between a business-as-usual Democratic Party and a Republican Party that ran on an agenda of specific reforms to the *system*.

The 1994 congressional election turned out to be a political earthquake of the first order, one whose aftershocks rumbled through Washington for years. The Democrats had been the dominant political party in this country since 1932. Indeed, in the sixty-two years after Franklin Roosevelt was first elected, the Republicans had control of the House of Representatives for only four years. More, in this federal Republic of fifty semisovereign states, "all politics is local," as former House Speaker Tip O'Neill frequently noted. And yet in 1994 not a single Republican incumbent running for reelection to the House, the Senate, or a governorship was defeated, while scores of Democrats, including numerous powerful committee chairmen, the putative next majority leader of the Senate, and even the sitting Speaker of the House, lost their offices (the last for the first time since the Civil War). It was one of the most singular events in the history of American politics, indicating a profound dissatisfaction on the part of the people with how the federal government was conducting the people's affairs.

As soon as the new Congress convened on January 3rd, 1995, it began making changes to the system. Many internal congressional reforms were enacted on the very first day of the new session, such as limiting the time that a member can hold a committee chairmanship, eliminating numerous subcommittees, and returning control over appointing committee chairmen to the Speaker, who was thereby given powerful leverage to keep the membership in line. And Congress finally subjected itself to the same rules that it had long imposed on the rest of the country, such as workplace safety regulations and sexual harassment laws, a clear change of course from the old "imperial Congress."

Far more important for the debt, however, Congress and the president acted to reverse the culture of spending as well. First, Congress finally passed a version of the line-item veto that allows presidents to strike out parts of an appropriations bill without vetoing the entire bill. And the line-item veto was granted by

a Republican Congress despite the fact that there was a Democrat in the White House. The very fact that Congress was finally
able to overcome the Madison Effect in order to serve the interests of the Republic is significant.

Presidents had been asking Congress for line-item veto authority since Ulysses S. Grant was in the White House, and it is a
power that is held by forty-three state governors. Interestingly, the
constitution of the Confederate States gave the President of the
Confederacy the power to "approve any appropriation and disap-
prove any other appropriation in the same bill." Such disapproval
could be overridden by the Confederate Congress.

Because it allows the president to veto not just an entire bill but
individual items within a bill, the line-item veto is a powerful political tool for controlling spending. With a line-item veto, the
executive can bargain much more effectively with individual
members of the legislature by threatening to veto an item a particular member wants, unless that member agrees to be with the
president to limit total spending.

In his State of the Union Address to Congress in 1985,
Ronald Reagan said, "Tonight I ask you to give me what forty-
three governors have: Give me a line-item veto this year. Give
me the authority to veto waste, and I'll take the responsibility, I'll
make the cuts, I'll take the heat." Ten years later, President Clinton echoed his predecessor's request.

The opposition to the line-item veto has been in two parts.
Some argued that it was simply unconstitutional, as the Constitu-
tion spells out in precise detail in the so-called Presentment Clause
(Article I, Section 7) how a bill shall become law and gives the
President the power to "return it with his Objections. . . ." This is

a classic strict-construction argument: If the Constitution doesn't specifically permit it, then it is forbidden.

Many more, however, objected not to the line-item veto's constitutionality but to the power shift over spending from Congress to the president that it would mean. Liberals, unions, and local officials, increasingly dependent on federal money, opposed it strenuously.

In the mid-1990s, however, with the results of the 1994 election still fresh in Washington, a Republican Congress voted to give a Democratic president a line-item veto. The bill was signed into law on April 9th, 1996, and immediately challenged in court by six senators, led by Robert Byrd of West Virginia, who claimed that it violated the Presentment Clause. A year later, a district federal judge agreed with the senators and struck down the law. But in 1997 the Supreme Court ruled that the senators lacked standing to sue and remanded the case back to the district court with instructions to dismiss it.

But when President Clinton began using the line-item veto (he would use it eleven times to strike eighty-two individual appropriations), those who were denied money, including the city of New York, sued. In February 1998, a district federal court struck down the act. In June of that year, the Supreme Court upheld the ruling, 6–3, in *Clinton v. City of New York*.

The majority opinion, written by Justice John Paul Stevens, one of the court's most liberal justices, took a strict-construction approach to the Presentment Clause. His opinion was joined by both liberal justices (such as David Souter) and conservative ones (such as Chief Justice William Rehnquist). The three dissenting justices, again made up of both liberals and conservatives, argued that the line-item veto was merely a lawful delegation of power to the executive and an efficient means by which a constitutional end might be achieved.

There was no chance of achieving the two-thirds majorities in each house of Congress to send a constitutional amendment allowing a line-item veto to the states (and no guarantee that three-quarters of the states—ever more dependent on federal revenue to balance their own budgets—would ratify it).

But despite the loss of the line-item veto, the budgetary situation of the federal government improved markedly in the late 1990s. The reason was twofold. First, it was a boom time in the American economy. Between 1990 and 2000, the gross domestic product increased by 69.2 percent. Thanks to a colossal boom on Wall Street in these years and to the progressive income tax, there was an even larger increase in federal revenues, which were 96.3 percent higher in 2000 than they had been a decade earlier. Second, the Republican-controlled Congress restrained spending. Federal outlays in 1990 were $1,253.1 trillion. A decade later they were $1,789.2 trillion, an increase of only 42.8 percent.

As a result, the federal budget was in "surplus" in 1998 for the first time since 1969, and stayed that way for the next three years. As we have seen, the surplus was an artifact of phony accounting. What was not an illusion was the decline in the debt as a percentage of GDP. In 1995 it was at 66.5 percent of GDP; by 2001 it had fallen to 57 percent.

Unfortunately, three factors combined to decisively change that trend as the new millennium dawned.

The first was the end of what came to be known as the dot-com bubble. As we have seen, the 1990s produced a great bull market on Wall Street, which resulted in the stock indexes reaching heights previously undreamed of. The Dow-Jones Industrial Average closed above the 1,000 mark for the first time in 1972 and closed below it for the last time in 1982. By the end of the 1990s, it closed at 11,497. But spectacular as the Dow-Jones's rise had been, it was nothing compared to the NASDAQ, which was heavy with smaller companies and, especially, high-tech ones.

The boundless promise of the Internet as a means of creating wealth had become manifest by the late 1990s and thousands of entrepreneurs developed business plans to exploit the new technology. Venture capitalists, who had been greatly empowered by the cuts in capital gains taxes enacted during the Clinton administration, funded these new firms and sold stock through IPOs (Wall Street jargon for Initial Public Offering). Investors, who could see the possibilities but not the problems inevitable in bringing those possibilities to fruition, bought these new stocks in an increasing frenzy. Price-earnings ratios of many of these stocks were, in fact, infinite as the new companies had no earnings at all, only business plans that, it was hoped, would produce earnings in the future.

The classic bubble that ensued was typical of what happens in the early days of a powerful new technology. Railroad stocks in the 1830s and airline stocks in the 1920s experienced similar if less frenzied bubbles. The NASDAQ, which had been under 400 as late as 1991 reached 1,000 by the middle of 1995 and 1,500 two years later. In late 1998 it stood at 2,000. Only fifteen months later, in March 2000, it reached 5,048.62.

At that point the bubble, as bubbles are wont to do, burst. The

NASDAQ lost half its value by the end of the year 2000 and by late in 2003 it stood at 1,114.11, a decline of 77.9 percent from its high three and half years earlier. This had a powerful impact on tax collections. The capital gains tax alone, which had raised $40 billion in federal revenues in 1995 had provided $121 billion in 2000. By 2003 capital gains tax receipts were only $45 billion.

A second factor affecting tax revenues were the events of September 11th, 2001. Insurance losses amounted to some $50 billion. Job losses in New York City amounted to 430,000, at least in the short term, and the city's GDP declined by $27 billion in the fifteen months following the attack on the World Trade Center. Federal revenues were also impacted, of course, and federal expenditures increased, with aid to New York City amounting to $11.2 billion in immediate aid and $10.5 billion the following year. Military expenditures to pay for the war in Afghanistan and, later, Iraq increased the Pentagon budget by 58 percent between fiscal 2001 and fiscal 2003.

The third factor was the slow but steady decline in Congress of the spending discipline that the Republican majority had brought following the 1994 election. Between 2001 and 2007, federal outlays increased by an astonishing 46 percent. President George Bush did not help. He did not veto a single bill until after Republicans lost control of Congress in 2006.

So-called earmarks have been an increasing part of the problem. In the ordinary appropriations process, Congress allows each federal department and agency to spend a given sum in the course of a fiscal year on general expenses and specified projects. The department then decides how best to use this money. With earmarks, Congress specifies not only the amount of money but exactly where and how and, often, by whom a particular project should be built. In other words, instead of allocating so much money for, say, bike trails, Congress requires the Department of the Interior to build a bike trail from A to B and to hire such and such a construction company to do the work. In fiscal 2008, there were over eleven thousand earmarks that appropriated a total of more than $17 billion.

The purpose of earmarks, of course, is to bring home the bacon to each congressman and senator's home district and state. Often the message is emphasized by requiring that the new facility be named for a particular congressman or senator. Senator Robert Byrd of West Virginia has no fewer than eleven major facilities named for him in his state. Representative John Murtha of Pennsylvania, the chairman of the Defense Appropriations subcommittee, is the namesake of a major commercial airport in his district. The airport is virtually unused, with only three flights a day. An $8 million state-of-the-art air traffic control radar system installed in 2004 remains unused for lack of need. The John Murtha Johnstown–Cambria County Airport is the poster child of all that is wrong with the earmark culture that has developed in Congress in recent years.

Seventeen billion dollars was only 5 percent of the total federal budget in fiscal 2008, but earmarks are a major symptom of what is wrong with Congress. The usual defense of earmarks is that members of Congress know what is best for their districts and state better than faceless bureaucrats in the executive branch. But the John Murtha Johnstown–Cambria County Airport cost $150 million to build and is used, on average, by twenty people a day. The three regular flights from the airport all go to Washington,

D.C. On one of them in April 2009, there were four passengers, whose six pieces of luggage were inspected by seven federal employees.

Earmarks, while not in themselves a major reason for the increases in the national debt, are what Senator Tom Coburn, Republican of Oklahoma, calls "the gateway drug to overspending." Earmarks have often been used as a means of getting members of Congress to vote for other, much greater spending bills they would otherwise have opposed.

And earmarks have been an engine of corruption. Representative Randall "Duke" Cunningham, Republican of California, pled guilty in 2005 to conspiracy to commit bribery, wire and mail fraud, and tax evasion. Among the evidence that convinced him to plead guilty was a piece of congressional stationery on which he had written the price, in bribes to him, for each million-dollar increase in the size of an earmarked government contract. Cunningham was sentenced to eight years and four months in prison and the forfeiture of $4.35 million in assets.

Regardless of the relentless increase in spending in the first decade of the twenty-first century, the annual on-budget deficit as a percentage of GDP declined rapidly after fiscal 2004. It was 3.4 percent in 2004, 2.5 percent in 2005, 1.9 percent in 2006, and 1.2 percent in 2007. Republicans, naturally, claim that this was due to the tax cuts that were enacted in 2001 and, especially, 2003, which Democrats (and the largely liberal media) dismissed as "tax cuts for the rich." Certainly tax revenues in the years 2003–2007 increased by 44 percent despite (or because of) the tax cuts. Had the spending discipline that had been in force during the late 1990s still been in force, the nominal federal budget would have returned to surplus. Of course, the nominal budget and the real budget were two different matters. The expenses of the wars in Iraq and Afghanistan were largely met by special, supplemental appropriations that were not part of the regular budget process. Thus they added to the national debt without appearing in the "deficit."

While the official deficit in fiscal 2004 was $412.7 billion, the national debt increased by $605 billion. In 2007 the deficit was $162 billion (1.2 percent of GDP) while the national debt rose $459.5 billion, a sum equal to 280 percent of the supposed deficit and 3.4 percent of GDP.

Then in 2008 all hell broke loose. In March of that year, Bear Stearns, the smallest of the major Wall Street investment firms, failed. It had been heavily invested in mortgage-backed securities and when the housing bubble that had been building through most of the 1990s and the early years of this century burst, Bear Stearns was unable to survive. At the heart of the housing bubble were two companies named the Federal National Mortgage Association and the Federal Home Loan Mortgage Association, universally known by their nicknames, Fannie Mae and Freddie Mac.

Fannie Mae was formed in 1938 as an agency of the federal government to add liquidity to the mortgage market. Fannie Mae's purpose was to buy up mortgages from initiating banks (freeing them to make more mortgages) and package these purchased mortgages as securities, selling them to investors or holding them in its own portfolio. As an agency of the federal government, Fannie Mae's obligations were backed by the full faith and credit of the United States.

Fannie Mae was one of the New Deal's better ideas and together with the GI Bill of 1944—which guaranteed mortgages for veterans—revolutionized home ownership in the United States. It had been rare for non-farm families to own their own homes in the 1930s. But the percentage that did so climbed steadily thereafter. It was 60 percent by the end of the 1960s and 64 percent by the 1980s. By owning a major financial asset, their own homes, millions of American families moved into the middle class. Fannie Mae helped mightily to transform this country from a country of haves and have-nots into a country of haves and have-mores.

One can argue that 64 percent is about as high as home ownership ought to go. Many young families are not yet ready to buy a home, many elderly people prefer to rent. Some people move too frequently for home ownership to make sense. And some people simply lack the creditworthiness that makes a bank willing to lend them money, even on the security of real property.

But home ownership had, by the 1990s, become almost a political fetish in Washington, an unalloyed good. In 1995, the Clinton administration rewrote the regulations regarding the enforcement of the Community Reinvestment Act of 1977. The act had originally been designed to eliminate racial discrimination in bank lending, called redlining, in which whole neighborhoods were denied mortgages, however creditworthy the people applying for the mortgage.* The new regulations virtually forced banks to seek out black customers and black neighborhoods, because they effectively if not explicitly established quotas for specific neighborhoods, spe-

---

* Ironically, it had not been the banks that had developed redlining, but the federal government itself. In 1935 the Federal Housing Administration, established the previous year to insure home mortgages thus making banks more willing to grant them, asked the Home Owner's Loan Corporation—still another New Deal agency, this one created to help prevent foreclosures—to

cific income classes, and specific races. One would think the banks would have fiercely resisted having to make loans to people they did not regard as good risks. They did not, because Fannie Mae was there to take over the risk. As long as they could offload the mortgage—and therefore the risk of default—the banks were willing to write these increasingly dubious mortgages and take the fees generated by doing so. Thus Fannie Mae created a huge moral hazard.

And by this point Fannie Mae had changed its nature. In 1968, as part of the Johnson administration's book cooking to make the federal budget deficit look lower, Fannie Mae had been spun off as a "Government Sponsored Enterprise" or GSE in Washington jargon. In theory, Fannie was now an independent company, its stock traded on the New York Stock Exchange no differently than, say, Citibank or Wells Fargo. In 1970, Freddie Mac was created theoretically to give Fannie competition, because other financial companies could not compete on a level playing field with Fannie.

While the legislation creating Fannie and Freddie explicitly denied it, everyone assumed (correctly as it turned out) that the government would not let either company fail. Thus they were able to continue to borrow at government, not bank, rates.

By the 1990s Fannie and Freddie were huge. By 2007 they were holding about half of the $12 trillion in outstanding

---

draw maps of residential areas according to the risk of lending in them. Affluent areas on these maps were outlined in blue, middle-class areas in yellow, poor neighborhoods in red. The FHA used these maps to determine which neighborhoods it would insure in and the banks, therefore, used the maps to determine the neighborhoods they would lend in.

mortgages in the country. That represented an enormous concentration of debt and of risk. Worse, Fannie and Freddie, unlike commercial banks, were able to invest up to forty times their capital in residential mortgages (banks can invest only ten times). Thus they quickly became grossly undercapitalized.

Many people, such as the editorial board of the *Wall Street Journal*, Alan Greenspan, chairman of the Federal Reserve, and President George W. Bush, recognized the danger and asked Congress to impose more stringent regulations and oversight on Fannie and Freddie. But Fannie and Freddie used their myriad political connections to thwart any additional regulation. Unlike any other major financial company, they are headquartered in Washington, D.C., and drew their top executives almost entirely from the Washington political establishment.

Fannie and Freddie could not buy so-called nonconforming mortgages, such as mortgages that were above a certain size (called jumbo mortgages) or certain subprime mortgages. Many banks moved into these areas aggressively and the number and variety of these mortgages increased greatly. There were adjustable-rate mortgages, teaser-rate mortgages that reset upward after a period, mortgages with no down payment, even mortgages with no questions asked regarding ability to repay.

Ever-rising housing prices—and they had been rising steadily since the Reagan years—it was said would protect the banks' interests. These subprime mortgages were bundled into complex securities and sold. The rating agencies, such as Standard & Poor, rated many of them highly, making them investment grade. Banks began holding these securities in their own portfolios, attracted by the high returns. In 1994, subprime mortgages made up 5 percent of all new mortgages, worth $35 billion. In 2006, they accounted for no less than 20 percent, worth $600 billion.

That year, the party began to end. Rising home prices had caused a surge in home building. The increased supply caused home prices to stall and then to begin falling. Those who had taken out adjustable-rate mortgages and those with teaser rates found they could not refinance before the rates reset. Defaults began to grow alarmingly, throwing the value of mortgage-based securities increasingly in doubt.

The collapse of Bear Stearns, which federal authorities arranged for J. P. Morgan Chase to take over, preventing default, proved a harbinger of a financial hurricane that struck in the fall of 2008. On September 7th, both Fannie and Freddie had to be placed under a federal conservatorship to prevent their default, their gargantuan debts guaranteed. On September 8th, Bank of America bought Merrill Lynch, which had faced losses of over $50 billion in subprime mortgage securities and almost certain failure.

A week later, Lehman Brothers, the third major Wall Street investment bank to fail in less than six months, declared bankruptcy. It was the largest bankruptcy in American history. The following day the Federal Reserve extended credit in the amount of $79 billion to prevent the collapse of the American International Group, the country's largest insurance firm, taking a warrant for nearly 80 percent of the company stock. The Federal Reserve, and the secretary of the Treasury, feared that the failure of AIG would set off a systemic collapse in the worldwide financial markets, with consequences no one could foresee.

Not surprisingly, the stock market crashed. The Dow Jones

Industrial Average lost nearly 2,500 points—22 percent—over the course of a week in early October and would drop another 2,000 points before finding a bottom in March 2009. Interest rates, meanwhile, soared as fear gripped financial markets.

The two remaining investment banks on Wall Street, Goldman Sachs and Morgan Stanley, took commercial bank charters, subjecting them to much more stringent regulation. In early October, Congress passed the Emergency Economic Stabilization Act of 2008, which authorized the Treasury to borrow up to $700 billion to buy troubled assets from commercial banks, in exchange for warrants that could be redeemed for common stock. Nineteen large banks took TARP (Troubled Assets Relief Program) funds. Many of them did not need the money, but the Treasury required them to do so for fear that people would otherwise shun the banks that did take these funds, causing the very collapse the funds were designed to prevent.

The TARP program and similar measures taken by other countries managed to stabilize the global financial system and it began to return to something approaching normal.

But the effect on the underlying economy, already in deepening recession, was severe, and it continued to contract sharply. The deficit in fiscal 2008, which ended September 30th of that year, was $410 billion, almost two and a half times what the deficit had been in 2007. The national debt in 2008, however, grew by $1.017 trillion, a staggering 7.4 percent of GDP.

In January 2009, the new Obama administration asked Congress for an $800 billion stimulus bill to keep the economy from stumbling further. President Obama argued that the infusion of such a large sum into the economy would keep unemployment, which had been rising rapidly, under 8 percent. Congress quickly passed a bill authorizing projects totaling $787 billion.

Unfortunately, President Obama left the details as to how the money would be allocated to Congress. Congress, with large Democratic majorities in both houses, used the bill as much to fund projects long on the liberal wish list as on projects that would stimulate the economy in the short term. Much of the stimulus money will not be spent until two and three years in the future. The bill received no Republican votes in the House and only three in the Senate.

Whether the stimulus bill would have worked had its allocations been directed entirely at stimulating the economy is an unanswerable question (although such Keynesian stimulus projects in the past have not worked well). And, in fact, unemployment kept rising despite the stimulus, reaching 10.2 percent in November 2009. Unemployment, however, is a lagging indicator, always recovering after the economy itself has started to move upward. There were numerous signs in the summer of 2009 that the worst of the recession was over and recovery was under way. The Dow Jones Industrial Average—always a powerful leading indicator—began to recover in March 2009.

But the deficit for fiscal 2009 reached a staggering $1.4 trillion dollars, by far the largest peacetime deficit, even adjusted for inflation, that the country has experienced in its history. At the end of fiscal 2008, the national debt amounted to 67.7 percent of GDP. At the end of fiscal 2009, it was 81 percent. That is by far the worst one-year increase in the debt-to-GDP ratio since the Second World War.

If President Obama's programs to limit carbon emissions and

reform health care are fully implemented by Congress, the Congressional Budget Office estimates that there will be deficits (according to the fundamentally dishonest federal accounting rules) over $600 billion each year for at least the next decade and that the actual national debt increases will be near a trillion dollars a year for the foreseeable future.

As the director of the CBO, Douglas Elmendorf, testified before a Senate committee in July 2009, "Under current law, the federal budget is on an unsustainable path—meaning that federal debt will continue to grow much faster than the economy over the long run. Although great uncertainty surrounds long-term fiscal projections, rising costs for health care and the aging of the U.S. population will cause federal spending to increase rapidly under any plausible scenario for current law. Unless revenues increase just as rapidly, the rise in spending will produce growing budget deficits and accumulating debt. Keeping deficits and debt from reaching levels that would cause substantial harm to the economy would require increasing revenues significantly as a percentage of gross domestic product (GDP), decreasing projected spending sharply, or some combination of the two."

Even a country as rich and productive as the United States can spend itself into bankruptcy as Spain did in the seventeenth century. Only fundamental change in how the government raises money, how and where it spends it, and how it accounts for it can prevent a future fiscal disaster.

CONCLUSION

In the 1860s we used the national debt to save the Union. In the 1930s we used it to save the American economy. In the 1940s we used it to save the world. So surely Hamilton was right, and the American national debt has been an immense national, indeed global, blessing. But is it still? Or is it now a crippling curse?

At the beginning of this book, I asked rhetorically if the current concern regarding the debt was overblown since we can well afford to service it and it is at 62 percent of the level, relative to GDP, of what it was at the end of World War II. I thought the answer to that question was no. Allow me to explain why.

Since it was established two hundred years ago, there have been seven periods in our history in which the national debt more or less steadily increased, six when it declined, and three when it was stable. Of the seven periods of increase, six were marked by either a major war or a depression. That is why the seventh period, the period since 1960, stands out in such stark contrast. For in the last fifty years we have had no more than ordinary fluctuations in the business cycle, and the wars we have fought, and are fighting, have been, relative to GDP, small wars.

Yet in this period we increased the size of the national debt by a factor of forty in nominal terms.

And for what? What have we saved—or gained—in exchange for imposing upon the future, generation after generation, interest costs of well over $1,800 *per person, per year*? The answer, I'm afraid, is little more than the political self-interests of a few thousand people, Democrats and Republicans alike, who held public office during this period. They were able, through a happenstantial confluence of economic theory and history, to use the national debt as a means of avoiding tough decisions—which are by definition unpopular with many. Resorting to increases in the debt rather than making those decisions was a short-term avoidance of political pain that will have long-term consequences that may well be much more painful, just as the excessive use of alcohol has short- and long-term consequences that are sharply at odds with each other.

And in fact, in recent years, Washington, wrestling with the budget deficit, has come to resemble more and more a drunk wrestling with alcoholism. First there is denial that there is a problem at all. The drunk claims that alcohol actually helps him function better. When that is no longer a tenable position, he makes deal after deal with himself to limit his drinking. He vows not to drink before 6 p.m., not to drink alone, not to drink anything stronger than wine. None of these deals work, of course, for more than a short time. His body now needs the alcohol, and he suspends his own self-imposed rules over and over again, but always "just this once." Finally, if he is lucky, there comes what is called an intervention, when his family and friends sit him down and tell him in no uncertain terms he needs help. If he listens, half the problem is solved.

If he doesn't, disaster is inevitable. The election of 1994 was, perhaps, an intervention. But if so, it didn't work for more than a few years. So, what is the next step? After all, it is not possible to send the federal government, or even its upper echelons, to a fiscal version of the Betty Ford Clinic.

It is, of course, the job of a historian to tell us how we got to where we are, not where we should go from here. But history also provides, in profligate abundance, examples of what not to do and lessons in how to proceed if success is to be possible. Let us look, briefly, at four such lessons, to be found in the history of the distribution of political power in society and that distribution's effects upon the checks and balances built into the Constitution; the history of political corruption; the history of accounting; and, finally, the alternatives to a tax system that history clearly shows has failed to achieve virtually all its objectives, both social and fiscal.

It was only in 1887 that Lord Acton coined his famous dictum that "power corrupts and absolute power corrupts absolutely." But exactly 100 years earlier, the Founding Fathers—the greatest practitioners of applied political science the world has yet produced—already had that truth firmly in mind when they wrote the Constitution. They realized intuitively that the pursuit of self-interest was a part of our unchangeable human nature and, indeed, the very reason that "men love power." Thus, to prevent the power they gave to one office from corrupting its occupant, they carefully checked and balanced it with the powers they gave to other offices. In this way they hoped to prevent the government from coming to serve the interests of the governors rather than the governed. In this they brilliantly succeeded, and the U.S. Constitution is, perhaps, the only work of genius ever created by a committee.

However, not even geniuses can foresee the future in its entirety. By giving Congress the sole power to appropriate money, the Founding Fathers thought they were checking the natural tendency of the executive to spend with the natural tendency of the most heavily taxed citizens to be frugal. In the context of the late eighteenth century, they were certainly correct, for at that time the wealthy class and the political class were, in large measure, the same. But the aristocrat-dominated world that the Founding Fathers assumed eternal—for it had been in place for untold generations—in fact began to break down almost immediately after they completed their task. Andrew Jackson, the first president of humble birth, then largely destroyed what was left of the aristocratic tradition in American politics.*

By 1840, being born rich was a fact that needed to be explained away or even lied about.†

---

* On the day of Jackson's inauguration, March 4th, 1829, an unprecedented number of ordinary citizens were in front of the Capitol (it was the first time the East Front was used for the ceremony) in order, wrote one contemporary, to witness the "triumph of the great principle of self government over the intrigues of the aristocracy." The White House reception that followed had in the past been restricted to "polite society." This time several thousand of what one witness called "a rabble, a mob, of boys, negros, women, children, scrambling, fighting, romping" jammed in and made an utter shambles of the place. They broke several thousand dollars worth of china and glassware, climbed on the furniture with muddy boots, and threatened Jackson's safety in their desire to get close to him. Finally Jackson had to escape, and servants brought the liquor out onto the lawn in order to get the people out of the White House.

† When William Henry Harrison ran for president in 1840, his campaign put out one of the earliest pieces of American political ephemera, a pocket

As people of ordinary means began to dominate Congress—and thus Congress began to spend "other people's money"—the tendency, even the ability, of Congress to be a check on spending began to evaporate. For as Calvin Coolidge, another notably frugal president, explained, "Nothing is easier than spending the public money. It does not appear to belong to anybody. The temptation is overwhelming to bestow it on somebody." Before long only the Smithian notion of fiscal prudence and the pre–New Deal concept of the limited role of the federal government kept spending in check. With the spread of Keynesianism, the slow transfer of power over the budget from the president to Congress, and the transformation of politics into a lifelong profession, Congress became the engine of spending, not the brake.

It is ironic, then, that the only logical brake today on the natural tendency of the modern Congress to spend is the presidency, the very office the Founding Fathers feared would be naturally profligate. The president is the one official in Washington—other than the powerless vice president—who is elected by the entire country and thus has his political self-interests directly bound up in the national interest of a prudent fiscal policy. This has been recognized by some for well over 100 years. What is needed to strike an effective balance between the president, who views the budget from a national, and personally unitary, vantage point, and Congress, which views it from 535 local perspectives?

---

handkerchief printed with scenes of Harrison's life. One scene showed his purported birthplace, a log cabin. In fact, Harrison had been born at his family's magnificent Berkeley Plantation on the James River in Virginia. Among countless other amenities, it had a front lawn large enough to encamp the entire Army of the Potomac in the Civil War.

One possibility would be to give the president the power to set the limit on overall spending, subject to a congressional override, and the power to enforce that limit with cuts in all spending, not just that specifically appropriated every year, as needed. Certainly Congress has shown itself, more than once, to be incapable of setting a limit to total spending and then sticking to it. If the president had the responsibility to set the limit on spending, the public would pay close attention to the figure he chose, a powerful incentive to choose wisely. This would require a constitutional amendment and thus the concurrence of two-thirds of each house of Congress. Only intense political pressure could induce Congress to cede such power to another branch of the government.

In the two hundred years since the present federal government was established, the concept of political corruption has changed profoundly. In the early days of the Republic, many sought political office precisely for the potential profits involved. In the 1830s, for instance, the great Daniel Webster, then a senator from Massachusetts, sent a private law client a bill for $500 for services rendered. The particular service in question, explicitly described in Webster's letter, was the insertion of an amendment into a piece of pending legislation, an amendment that greatly benefited the client. In Webster's day that was simply business as usual; today, of course, it is a felony.

The shift in attitude toward such behavior began when a brand-new player entered onto the political stage, at about the same time that Webster was sending his bill. Until the 1830s, newspapers had been both small in circulation and fiercely partisan in their politics.

But James Gordon Bennett invented the mass media when he launched the *New York Herald* in 1835, a newspaper that was both politically independent and aimed at a large and general audience. Bennett began reporting the activities of politicians with an eye to the news value, not the politics, of the situation, and public opinion quickly forced a change in what was regarded as acceptable.

The politicians, of course, deprived of a steady source of income, resisted the change. In the late 1860s the thoroughly corrupt New York state legislature passed a law stating that a conviction for bribery could be had only on the testimony of a third party. In the preelectronic era, of course, that meant that as long as an official took his bribe in cash and in privacy there was no possibility of his being called to account. In effect, then, the legislature legalized bribery. The law was repealed after the fall of the so-called Tweed Ring (brought down when the *New York Times* published massive evidence of corruption in the city and state governments) in 1871. A new law regarding the bribing of public officials was then put into the state constitution, where the legislature could not easily change it.

Although there will always be crooks in government, we have come a long way from the days of Boss Tweed and our politics are cleaner today than they have ever been before, despite a steady trickle of indicted members of Congress. It is ironic, therefore, that in the last forty years the PAC system of financing political campaigns has come into its own. For this system is legal bribery and nothing but. Just consider. The only difference between an illegal bribe and a PAC contribution is that the latter lacks an explicit quid pro quo. But there is always an implicit one. As Charles Keating, who served four and a half years in jail for wire and bankruptcy fraud in the savings-and-loan scandal, replied when asked if his PAC contributions had brought him influence, "I certainly hope so." Indeed, to buy influence is the only reason corporations, unions, and other interest groups give PAC contributions to politicians.

That is why the PAC system of financing political campaigns must be abolished. It cannot be reformed any more than slavery could have been reformed and for precisely the same reason: It is inherently morally corrupt. And as long as it exists, it will exert a steady and by no means minor pressure to increase federal spending over and above what it would otherwise be. It is only a slight exaggeration to say that behind every "earmark" is a PAC contribution. It is doubtful that any member of Congress has ever received a PAC contribution from an organization seeking to cut government spending. To use the alcoholism analogy again, as long as the PAC system exists, there will be tens of thousands of lobbyists in Washington whispering into the ear of every member of Congress, "Let's have a drink. One little beer can't hurt."

What should replace the current system of campaign finance? McCain-Feingold and other attempts to get money out of politics have been dismal failures (trying to get money out of politics, after all, is a bit like trying to get sex out of procreation) or incumbent protection acts. Campaigns cost more than ever and incumbents can much more easily raise money under present law than can opponents. Instead, four rules would greatly improve the situation. 1) No cash, traceable contributions only. 2) Only individuals may contribute. 3) No foreigners. 4) Instant and full disclosure. The same day that the check is deposited should be the day that the check writer's name and association goes up on the campaign Web site. Reporters can be counted on to patrol those Web sites closely, looking for patterns that indicate excess influence.

It is seldom noticed—perhaps because accounting induces instant narcolepsy in most nonaccountants—but the development of accounting was one of the great intellectual achievements of Western civilization. Indeed, the modern world would be quite impossible without it.

Accounting did not advance much beyond the techniques used by the Mesopotamians until that intellectual explosion known as the Italian Renaissance produced double-entry bookkeeping in the fifteenth century. Double entry makes it much easier to detect errors and allows a much more dynamic financial picture of an enterprise to emerge from the raw numbers. Thus the difference between double-entry and single-entry bookkeeping as financial tools might be analogous to the difference between an electrocardiogram and a stethoscope as diagnostic ones.

Accountants, armed with the new methods, came early to the New World. In fact, Isabella and Ferdinand put one on board the *Santa Maria* in 1492 to make sure that they got their full share of the hoped-for booty. But American enterprises remained very small until well after the Revolution. Their owners did most of their own bookkeeping and were often self-taught, out of such books as *Book-keeping Methodiz'd: or A methodical treatise of Merchant-Accompts, according to the Italian form*, published in 1718. So although professional accountants, working for a variety of clients, existed (Benjamin Franklin used one occasionally to help keep track of his numerous enterprises), they were not common.

Nor were they independent in the sense that they certified

books as being correct. They didn't need to be because American enterprises were nearly always individually owned so there was no reason for anyone to keep dishonest books.

The Industrial Revolution, however, changed that forever. The railroads were the first industry with capital needs beyond the means of a single person or family. And they soon concatenated into lines stretching hundreds and then thousands of miles, and began selling their securities on Wall Street to people who took no part in their management.

As these enterprises became more and more complex, accountants began devising more and more tools to keep track of the money and to enable the managers to see exactly where and how it was being spent (or misspent). The great corporate enterprises of the late nineteenth century were only possible because of these new accounting tools, and this rapid evolution in accountancy continues unabated today. Cash flow, for instance, is now one of the most important numbers an accountant produces, yet the term was not coined until 1954.

But as the distance between the owners of the railroads—the stockholders—and the managers who ran them (and kept the books) increased steadily, the interests of the owners and managers with regard to those books diverged as well. The owners wanted timely information that would allow them to evaluate the worth of their holdings and to compare them with other, similar concerns, in order to determine how good a job the managers were doing. The managers, naturally, wanted the freedom to make the books look as good as possible, and, because much of bookkeeping is inherently arbitrary, they had the freedom to do so. Sometimes, of course, the managers went beyond a self-serving choice of accounting methods and lurched into fraud.

Many publicly traded companies did not release figures at all. Even when a railroad issued a report, a contemporary wrote, it was "often a very blind document, and the average shareholder . . . generally gives up before he begins." The Erie Railway, for instance, because some of its many bond issues were backed by New York State, was required to file an annual report with Albany. But the editor Horace Greeley, in 1870, harrumphed in the *New York Tribune* that if the new annual report of the Erie Railway was accurate, then "Alaska has a tropical climate and strawberries in their season."

The Commercial and Financial Chronicle, the *Barron's* of its day, put its finger on the solution when it called for all companies to issue regular quarterly reports, "showing the sources and amounts of its revenues, the disposition made of every dollar, the earnings of its property, the expenses of working, of supplies, of new construction, and of repairs, the amount and form of its debt, and the disposition made of all its funds."

Today quarterly and annual reports are so much a part of the capitalist world that it is hard to imagine that only 125 years ago they were a brand-new idea. Wall Street immediately realized how important such reports could be in evaluating securities. Henry Clews, a very influential broker in the post–Civil War era, led the push for both regular reports and, equally important, independent accountants to certify them. The great Wall Street bankers such as J. P. Morgan, who were becoming more and more vital to the new industrial corporations, joined him, as did the New York Stock Exchange. The managers did not like the idea, of course, but if they wanted to raise capital or have their securities listed on the country's only important stock exchange, they had little choice.

In the 1880s the number of independent accountants began to increase rapidly. In 1884 there were only eighty-one accountants listed in the city directories of New York, Chicago, and Philadelphia combined. Just five years later, there were 322. In 1896 New York State passed legislation establishing the legal basis of the profession and, incidentally, used the term *certified public accountant* for the first time to designate those who met the criteria of the law. The legislation, and the term, were quickly copied by the other states.

By the First World War, the days when the managers of a publicly held corporation could keep the numbers secret or make themselves look good with carefully selected methods of bookkeeping were long gone, and independent accountants were applying GAAP—Generally Accepted Accounting Principles—to all publicly traded companies. It has proved to be one of capitalism's better ideas.

Government, however, has been largely unaffected by this revolution in accountancy. As we have seen, the federal government did not even have a formal budget process until 1922. Virtually all federal accounting is still oriented toward preventing fraud and theft, not toward controlling costs. Indeed, Congress has several times actually forbidden federal agencies to analyze the cost-effectiveness of programs in order to avoid the political heat of maintaining those that don't work well. To this day the government makes no attempt to determine even so basic a measure of efficiency as the overhead of any of its vast array of departments, bureaus, and agencies. And the U.S. government still doesn't use double-entry bookkeeping. It keeps its books the way you and I keep our checkbooks.

The Founding Fathers understood that where there is a conflict of interest, there will be corruption, either moral or legal, but the one device that ensures honest books—independent certifying accountants—had not yet been invented. So while the Constitution requires that "a regular Statement of Account of the receipts and Expenditures of all public Money shall be published from time to time," it was left up to the government to decide how to design that statement. The "managers" of government have been no more self-serving about doing so than the managers of nineteenth-century corporations were. But neither have they been less self-serving.

This is why one frequently proposed solution to the continuing budget deficits, the Balanced Budget Amendment, is, in fact, a chimera: It is easier to use accounting gimmicks than it is to make hard political choices. Consider just one recent example: New York State, in 1992, found itself $200 million short of the money needed to balance its expense budget, which the state constitution requires be funded out of current income. Did the legislature and the governor raise taxes or cut spending to achieve the mandated balance? Certainly not. Instead, the state of New York simply sold Attica State Prison to itself.

The Urban Development Corporation, a state agency established to help redevelop troubled urban areas, borrowed in the bond market, turned the money over to the state, and took title to the prison. The state, in turn, recorded the $200 million its own agency had borrowed as income, proclaimed the budget balanced, and now rents Attica from the UDC at a price sufficient to service the debt created.

The federal government regularly indulges in similar, if perhaps not quite so blatant, accounting shenanigans. As we have seen, the Social Security Trust Fund has been both on and off the budget depending on whether it was operating in surplus or deficit at the time and thus would make the total budget deficit look better or worse.

Further, the federal government currently operates on a cash basis, much as a child's lemonade stand does. Income is recorded only as received, and outlays are recorded only when the checks are actually written. Meanwhile, the government makes no distinction between, say, meeting the navy's payroll, which is an expense, and paying for an aircraft carrier, which is an investment.

All this is extremely convenient for politicians, because they can enact programs now, and get the political credit for them, while worrying about actually paying for them later. In this way, the federal government has many trillions of dollars of future obligations—in Social Security payments, Medicare, Medicaid, employee pension benefits, veteran benefits, etc.—that are not accounted for and for which no provision is being made. (The federal government, however, regulates corporate and union pension funds and requires that they be properly funded.) As these obligations increasingly come due as the population ages, the crunch on the federal budget will be increasingly onerous. The Medicare trust fund will be exhausted in less than ten years, the Social Security Trust Fund in less than forty. This is essentially a fiscal time bomb that will detonate in the coming decades. And unlike economic predictions, the predictions regarding these obligations are demographic and thus highly reliable. After all, everyone who will be entitled to these obligations by 2050 is already alive.

Alexander Hamilton realized two centuries ago that politicians could not be trusted with the power to print money, because they would always be tempted to solve their immediate fiscal problems by resorting to the printing press, and all too often succumb to that temptation. One hundred years ago, J. P. Morgan and others realized that managers of large corporations could not be trusted to keep non-self-serving books. Today the "managers" of the federal government cannot be trusted to keep them either and for exactly the same reason: They are human.

Of course, no one would argue that the books of a sovereign power can be kept like those of a profit-seeking corporation. There is no quantifying the value of Yellowstone National Park, or objectively determining the worth of foreign aid or the Head Start program. Those are political decisions, not bookkeeping ones. But the books should be kept consistently and in ways that illuminate, not obscure, the true picture; reveal, not conceal, if the managers have succeeded or failed in their jobs.

The Congressional Budget Office, which is nonpartisan, could be empowered to establish rigorous and transparent accounting standards for the Treasury. Another approach, even more independent of the political branches, would be to establish an accounting board modeled on the structure of the Federal Reserve (which, in fact, is where the power to print money is now vested). The members would be appointed to long, staggered terms to insulate them from politics, and they would have a duty, just as CPAs do, to keep the books honestly and consistently according to recognized principles. This entity might well also take over many of the functions, now duplicated by the Office of Management and Budget and the Congressional Budget Office, to estimate revenues and analyze the fiscal impact of changes in taxes and spending, two areas where political considerations are most prone to influence what are, at best, guesstimates anyway.

Unfortunately, the "stockholders" in this case have no J. P. Morgan at their disposal to impose such a change in the status quo, and the "managers" are going to resist it furiously, thanks to the Madison Effect. Indeed, the very fact that this obvious problem has been completely left out of the political discussion regarding the deficit is evidence of just how central it is to the solution. There can be no serious reform of the federal budget process until control over keeping the books is taken away from politicians. After all, despite New York State's constitutional requirement that its budget be balanced, there was nothing except shame—which was obviously insufficient—to keep the state from selling an asset to itself and calling it income. Even New York State realizes what is needed, not that Albany has imposed it upon itself. In the 1970s, when New York City went broke, the state wouldn't help until the city accepted a financial control board and adopted GAAP for keeping its books.

The effect on the country's fiscal policy, and thus on the debt, of proper books would be considerable. First, proper accounting is a powerful instrument for rooting out waste. Second, history is full of examples of government programs that start small and are projected to remain so but mushroom into vast ones. NASA has frequently underestimated the costs of particular projects, most notably the space shuttle, knowing that once Congress has committed billions to a project it will be reluctant to abandon it when it goes way over budget. When Medicare was started in 1965, it was estimated that its costs in 1990 would be $9 billion. In fact they were ten times greater. In fiscal 2008, Medicare spending was $413 billion, larger than all but a handful of federal expenses and up 2.8 times in inflation-adjusted dollars from 1990. And, again, look at New York. It is intrinsically one of the richest states in the Union, but it has a nearly forty-year history of budget gimmicks and the second-lowest credit rating of any state.

Karl Marx's prescription for dealing with the inequities of the European economy of the 1840s was very high marginal rates on large incomes. This remains the preferred tax system of the political left despite a near-ninety-year history in the United States that demonstrates beyond any doubt that its results are economically and politically perverse in a democratic society. As we have seen, even as early as the Wilson administration, which put the modern federal income tax in place in 1913, it was obvious that the rich could (and would) avoid the high rates by exploiting loopholes and influencing Congress to increase the number of loopholes as rates go up.

The result has been a tax system of unbelievable complexity that doesn't even accomplish the goal of forcing the rich to pay more of their income in taxes than those less fortunate. Warren Buffett famously noted that he pays 17 percent of his income in taxes while his assistant pays 35 percent. Further, a tax system that is dependent on a small part of the population at the top of the income spectrum will always be highly volatile. In boom times, revenues flow into the federal Treasury as well as those states, such as California and New York, with high income tax rates, tempting politicians to increase government services and programs. But in the inevitable bust that follows, tax revenues plummet and budgetary crises follow.

What are the alternatives? Some advocate eliminating the two income taxes altogether and substituting a sales taxes. The VAT tax, popular in Europe, taxes goods and services at every level of production, and these taxes are then built into the final price. There are two disadvantages to a VAT tax. First, it is complicated and requires a lot of expensive accounting by corporations, which violates Adam Smith's fourth principle of taxation that "every tax ought to be so contrived as both to take out and to keep out of the pockets of the people as little as possible, over and above what it brings into the public treasury." And the tax is hidden, making it easier for politicians to raise it without full public consensus.

A national sales tax would not be hidden (it would show up on every sales slip), but being a consumption tax (the VAT is, too), it would not tax much of the incomes of the very rich and is thus inherently regressive. It has the very same drawback as the nineteenth-century tax system of tariffs and excises, violating Smith's first principle of taxation that "the subjects of every state ought to contribute towards the support of the government . . . in proportion to the revenue which they respectively enjoy under the protection of the state."

What's left, then, is a flat tax, which taxes every dime earned above a personal exemption by allowing no deductions, credits, or any other of the myriad complications that have grown on the tax code over the last ninety years like barnacles. Further, all proposed flat taxes merge the corporate and personal income tax systems, thus taxing all income but taxing it only once while preventing the rich (and the politicians doling out favors to the rich in exchange for campaign contributions) from using the interaction of the two systems for their own advantage. Because there are no complications, both individuals and companies could fill out their income taxes on the back of a postcard. And because there are no deductions, politicians would not be able to hide social and economic engineering, or political favors, in the tax code, where they don't belong.

History clearly shows that tax deductions and credits are to politicians what cocktails are to alcoholics: It is a lot easier for them to refuse the first one than the second. Just in the ten years after the 1986 major simplification of the tax code under the leadership of President Reagan and House Ways and Means Committee chairman Dan Rostenkowski, for instance, the code was amended no fewer than *4,000* times, a rate better than one amendment a day. The vast majority of these amendments were nothing more than political favors to powerful individuals and interest groups.

There are two main criticisms of a flat tax. The first is that it is, well, flat: There is no progressivity. But that is simply not true. The *marginal* rate—the amount of tax on the next dollar of income earned—is, indeed, flat. But it should be. Otherwise the rich man is more discouraged than the poor man from earning that next dollar—something he is obviously good at—and the government cannot tax a dollar that has not been earned. What is not flat is the *effective* tax rate, the amount of total income that is taken in taxes.

Here is a simple illustration: Assume a $10,000 personal exemption and a 20 percent tax rate on all income above that amount. Under those conditions, a family of four would have a 0 percent effective tax rate at an income of $40,000, but a 4 percent rate at $50,000. If the family's income were $100,000, its effective tax rate would be 12 percent, and at $1 million 19.2 percent of the family's income would be taxed away. Thus, with a flat tax, you know that however much you are paying, the guy down the block who is making more money than you is paying not only more taxes but a higher percentage of his total income in taxes as well. Today you only know that he probably has a better tax accountant.

The other criticism is that the flat tax would hit the middle class harder than it would the rich, compared with the present system. But this is only true if one compares the personal part of many flat tax proposals with today's personal income tax. The integrated flat tax must be compared with both the personal and the corporate income taxes together to get a true picture. After all, how much higher would stock dividends be if the corporations that pay them passed on the income tax liability on profits to the stockholders? How much more restrained would be the now-myriad perks that are used to give corporate managers untaxed income if the corporations could no longer deduct them as business expenses?

Corporations are nothing more than wealth-creating machines established for the benefit of their stockholders. And the various proposals for a flat tax would all tax them much as they would tax individuals. In other words, no deductions beyond the direct cost of doing business and at the same rate. There would be no more shifting of income between corporate and personal in order to gain tax advantages.

Nor would a flat tax interfere with the politics of taxation regarding how much of the burden should be borne by what economic segments of the population and how much to tax. A liberal administration and Congress might raise the personal exemption and increase the tax rate to compensate. That would move the burden sharply up the economic scale, giving tax relief to those lower down while maintaining tax revenues. A conservative government might lower the marginal rate to stimulate capital formation and make up the lost revenue in spending cuts. In the event of an emergency, such as war, a lowering of the personal exemption combined with an increase in the tax rate would send government revenues soaring while sharply curbing civilian demands on the economy by absorbing disposable income.

What would *not* be possible would be using the tax code to dispense political favors. That, of course, is precisely why so many politicians, of the right, left, and center, resist the very concept of a flat tax: It would sharply curtail their power to make political bargains. The greatest enemy of the flat tax is the Madison Effect.

But from the point of view of fiscal policy, the greatest advantage of the flat tax, and also an advantage of the various sales and VAT taxes, is that it would be possible to predict with some degree of accuracy the revenue effects of changing tax rates, because the rate chosen would impact equally on everyone rich enough to be taxed at all and there would be nowhere to shift revenue in order to avoid or postpone taxes.

From the point of view of the debt, the ability to reliably predict revenues from a given tax rate would make it possible to reliably know how much spending could be allowed without having to borrow. Thus if it were decided to utilize the national debt, it would be for a given amount and a given reason. The current tax system allows politicians to use rosy revenue assumptions to justify politically useful spending.

Alexander Hamilton conceived of the national debt as a strategic instrument of national policy to be used to protect and advance the interests of the nation. In the last several decades, however, it has not been used for that purpose. Rather, it has become nothing more than an escape valve for political pressure. As such, it has served not the strategic interests of the nation but the day-to-day interests of politicians. If this continues for very much longer, not only will the strategic interests of the country not be served, they will be gravely injured.

For we cannot borrow the same dollar twice unless we pay it back first. And it should be kept in mind that we no longer are borrowing just from ourselves, as Lord Keynes thought we would. Today 25 percent of the national debt is held by foreigners. Any loss of faith by these foreign bond holders regarding the country's ability or intent to service its debt would have very serious consequences, for the interest rates the Treasury pays to borrow money would increase sharply if foreign buyers dropped out of the market. At the close of the 2009 fiscal year, on September 30th of that year, the national debt stood at $11.807 trillion. That's $1.683 trillion, 16.6 percent, higher than one year earlier. The debt at the end of fiscal 2009 was rising at the rate of $1 million every twenty seconds. That's $180 million every hour, $4.320 billion every day, $129.6 billion just in the month of September.

To be sure, the country has endured a bad recession, and economic downturns always reduce tax revenues while increasing such government expenses as unemployment benefits, food stamps, and other programs to relieve poverty. But the Obama administration now projects that the national debt will continue to expand even with the return of economic growth.

Indeed, it projects a near doubling of the debt by the year 2015 to $20 trillion. The administration estimates that the debt will reach 100 percent of GDP in 2010 and then remain at that level as the economy resumes growth. But that is predicated on projected annual growth of GDP ranging from 2.6 percent to 4.6 percent, well above the average prediction of private-sector economists. If growth is less robust, or another recession should hit, then the debt as a percentage of GDP will continue to climb, perhaps to levels only reached at the end of World War II.

As of this writing, the national debt remains a blessing, available to mobilize the titanic economic resources of the United States in order to meet any conceivable emergency. But for it to remain so and not become a curse, as Spain's debt did in the sixteenth and seventeenth centuries, the way business is done in Washington needs to be radically overhauled. The status quo is a sure-fire recipe for fiscal disaster in the not too distant future.

The now-forty-year-long string of significant annual budget deficits, incurred in mostly good times and largely for the purpose of ensuring the reelection of members of Congress (of all parties and political philosophies) constitutes overwhelming evidence that the system is irretrievably broken. It must be made anew.

To accomplish this we must elect to office men and women committed to putting in place new rules, rules that take into account the economic and political realities that emerged in the twentieth century. These rules must, like those devised by the

Founding Fathers, force politicians to pursue their short-term self-interests in reelection in ways that advance the long-term public interest in a prudent fiscal policy.

This will be no easy task, of course, for the people who will, in the end, devise and put in place the new rules, are the very people whose self-interests have been most directly protected by the current ones: politicians themselves. And one reality no one can change is the Madison Effect. But recent events have shown that even that can be overcome by a determined electorate. So while it will be a bruising political battle, it is one we must fight, not only for our sake, but even more for the sake of our grandchildren.

APPENDIX

The Statistics

The data in these tables come from the two-volume *Historical Statistics of the United States: Colonial Times to 1970*, published by the U.S. Department of Commerce in 1975 for the bicentennial. More recent data come from the *Statistical Abstract of the United States*, published annually by the Commerce Department.

The careful reader will surely note discrepancies in these numbers, which is not surprising given the complexity of the federal budget. The discrepancies, however, are relatively small and, for the purposes of this book, of no significance, since these statistics are intended solely to illuminate the distinctly macroscaled story of the national debt. Let me attempt some explanation nonetheless.

Each set of data is not wholly consistent with itself, as the exact accounting definitions of revenues, outlays, surplus and deficit, and the total debt have all changed several times in the two hundred years of the debt's existence. For instance, before 1913, receipts were total receipts; since then they have been net receipts. Further, the end of the federal fiscal year changed from December 31st to

June 30th in 1843 and to September 30th in 1976. And the United States Government has sometimes incurred obligations for reasons other than financing a deficit, such as railroad development in the nineteenth century and the TVA in the 1930s. A particularly interesting discrepancy occurs in 1803. That year a surplus of more than $3 million was recorded, yet the national debt actually grew by more than $9 million. This apparent contradiction makes sense with the knowledge that 1803 was the year the United States bought the Louisiana Purchase from France for $15 million in bonds and claim settlements, an expense not carried as a normal outlay for obvious reasons.

To add to the confusion, because of these and, doubtless, other reasons the sets of data are also not wholly consistent with each other. For instance, as early as 1798, when federal revenues for that year are officially given as $7,900,000 and outlays as $7,677,000, one would think that the surplus would have been $223,000. But it is given as $224,000. Exactly why this and other even larger annual discrepancies should be, I confess I haven't the faintest idea.

Federal Debt Statistics

YEAR	REVENUES	OUTLAYS	ANNUAL SURPLUS (DEFICIT)	DEBT AS % OF GNP/GDP	ACCUMULATED NATIONAL DEBT
1792	3,670,000	5,080,000	−1,410,000		80,359,000
1793	4,653,000	4,482,000	171,000		78,427,000
1794	5,432,000	6,991,000	−1,559,000		80,748,000

YEAR	REVENUES	OUTLAYS	ANNUAL SURPLUS (DEFICIT)	DEBT AS % OF GNP/GDP	ACCUMULATED NATIONAL DEBT
1795	6,115,000	7,540,000	−1,425,000		83,762,000
1796	8,378,000	5,727,000	2,651,000		82,064,000
1797	8,689,000	6,134,000	2,555,000		79,229,000
1798	7,900,000	7,677,000	224,000		78,409,000
1799	7,547,000	9,666,000	−2,120,000		82,976,000
1800	10,849,000	10,786,000	63,000		83,038,000
1801	12,935,000	9,395,000	3,541,000		80,713,000
1802	14,996,000	7,862,000	7,134,000		77,055,000
1803	11,064,000	7,852,000	3,212,000		86,427,000
1804	11,826,000	8,719,000	3,107,000		82,312,000
1805	13,561,000	10,506,000	3,055,000		75,723,000
1806	15,560,000	9,804,000	5,756,000		69,218,000
1807	16,398,000	8,354,000	8,044,000		65,196,000
1808	17,061,000	9,932,000	7,129,000		57,023,000
1809	7,773,000	10,281,000	−2,508,000		53,173,000
1810	9,384,000	8,157,000	1,227,000		48,006,000
1811	14,424,000	8,058,000	6,366,000		45,210,000
1812	9,801,000	20,281,000	−10,480,000		55,963,000
1813	14,340,000	31,682,000	−17,342,000		81,488,000
1814	11,182,000	34,721,000	−23,539,000		99,834,000
1815	15,729,000	32,708,000	−16,979,000		127,335,000
1816	47,678,000	30,587,000	17,091,000		123,492,000
1817	33,099,000	21,844,000	11,255,000		103,467,000
1818	21,585,000	19,825,000	1,760,000		95,530,000
1819	24,603,000	21,464,000	3,139,000		91,016,000
1820	17,881,000	18,261,000	−380,000		89,987,000
1821	14,573,000	15,811,000	−1,238,000		93,547,000
1822	20,232,000	15,000,000	5,232,000		90,876,000
1823	20,541,000	14,707,000	5,834,000		90,270,000
1824	19,381,000	20,327,000	−946,000		83,788,000
1825	21,841,000	15,857,000	5,984,000		81,054,000
1826	25,260,000	17,036,000	8,224,000		73,987,000
1827	22,966,000	16,139,000	6,827,000		67,475,000
1828	24,764,000	16,395,000	8,369,000		58,421,000
1829	24,828,000	15,203,000	9,625,000		48,565,000
1830	24,844,000	15,143,000	9,701,000		39,123,000
1831	28,527,000	15,248,000	13,279,000		24,322,000
1832	31,866,000	17,289,000	14,577,000		7,012,000

YEAR	REVENUES	OUTLAYS	ANNUAL SURPLUS (DEFICIT)	DEBT AS % OF GNP/GDP	ACCUMULATED NATIONAL DEBT
1833	33,948,000	23,018,000	10,930,000		4,760,000
1834	21,792,000	18,628,000	3,164,000		38,000
1835	35,430,000	17,573,000	17,857,000		38,000
1836	50,827,000	30,868,000	19,959,000		337,000
1837	24,954,000	37,243,000	−12,289,000		3,308,000
1838	26,303,000	33,865,000	−7,562,000		10,434,000
1839	31,483,000	26,899,000	4,584,000		3,573,000
1840	19,480,000	24,318,000	−4,838,000		5,251,000
1841	16,860,000	26,566,000	−9,706,000		13,594,000
1842	19,976,000	25,206,000	−5,230,000		20,201,000
1843	8,303,000	11,858,000	−3,555,000		32,743,000
1844	29,321,000	22,338,000	6,983,000		23,462,000
1845	29,970,000	22,937,000	7,033,000		15,925,000
1846	29,700,000	27,767,000	1,933,000		15,550,000
1847	26,496,000	57,281,000	−30,785,000		38,827,000
1848	35,736,000	45,377,000	−9,641,000		47,045,000
1849	31,208,000	45,052,000	−13,844,000		63,062,000
1850	43,603,000	39,543,000	4,060,000		63,453,000
1851	52,559,000	47,709,000	4,850,000		68,305,000
1852	49,847,000	44,195,000	5,652,000		66,199,000
1853	61,587,000	48,184,000	13,403,000		59,805,000
1854	73,800,000	58,045,000	15,755,000		42,244,000
1855	65,351,000	59,743,000	5,608,000		35,588,000
1856	74,057,000	69,571,000	4,486,000		31,974,000
1857	68,965,000	67,796,000	1,169,000		28,701,000
1858	46,655,000	74,185,000	−27,530,000		44,913,000
1859	53,486,000	69,071,000	−15,585,000		58,498,000
1860	56,065,000	63,131,000	−7,066,000		64,844,000
1861	41,510,000	66,547,000	−25,037,000		90,582,000
1862	51,987,000	474,762,000	−422,775,000		524,178,000
1863	112,697,000	714,741,000	−602,044,000		1,119,774,000
1864	264,627,000	865,323,000	−600,696,000		1,815,831,000
1865	333,715,000	1,297,555,000	−963,840,000		2,677,929,000
1866	558,033,000	520,809,000	37,224,000		2,755,764,000
1867	490,634,000	357,543,000	133,091,000		2,650,168,000
1868	405,638,000	377,340,000	28,298,000		2,583,446,000
1869	370,944,000	322,865,000	48,079,000		2,545,111,000
1870	411,255,000	309,654,000	101,601,000		2,436,453,000

YEAR	REVENUES	OUTLAYS	ANNUAL SURPLUS (DEFICIT)	DEBT AS % OF GNP/GDP	ACCUMULATED NATIONAL DEBT
1871	383,324,000	292,177,000	91,147,000		2,322,052,000
1872	374,107,000	277,518,000	96,589,000		2,209,991,000
1873	333,738,000	290,345,000	43,393,000		2,151,210,000
1874	304,979,000	302,634,000	2,345,000		2,159,933,000
1875	288,000,000	274,623,000	13,377,000		2,156,277,000
1876	294,096,000	265,101,000	28,995,000		2,130,846,000
1877	281,406,000	241,334,000	40,072,000		2,107,760,000
1878	257,764,000	236,964,000	20,800,000		2,159,418,000
1879	273,827,000	266,948,000	6,879,000		2,298,913,000
1880	333,527,000	267,643,000	65,884,000		2,090,909,000
1881	360,782,000	260,713,000	100,069,000		2,019,286,000
1882	403,525,000	257,981,000	145,544,000		1,856,916,000
1883	398,288,000	265,408,000	132,880,000		1,721,959,000
1884	348,520,000	244,126,000	104,394,000		1,625,307,000
1885	323,691,000	260,227,000	63,464,000		1,578,551,000
1886	336,440,000	242,483,000	93,957,000		1,555,660,000
1887	371,403,000	267,932,000	103,471,000		1,465,485,000
1888	379,266,000	267,925,000	111,341,000		1,384,632,000
1889	387,050,000	299,289,000	87,761,000	10.00%	1,249,471,000
1890	403,081,000	318,041,000	85,040,000	8.57%	1,122,397,000
1891	392,612,000	365,774,000	26,838,000	7.45%	1,005,807,000
1892	354,938,000	345,023,000	9,915,000	6.76%	968,219,000
1893	385,820,000	383,478,000	2,342,000	6.97%	961,432,000
1894	306,355,000	367,525,000	−61,170,000	8.07%	1,016,898,000
1895	324,729,000	356,195,000	−31,466,000	7.89%	1,096,913,000
1896	338,142,000	352,179,000	−14,037,000	9.19%	1,222,729,000
1897	347,722,000	365,774,000	−18,052,000	8.40%	1,226,794,000
1898	405,321,000	443,369,000	−38,048,000	8.00%	1,232,743,000
1899	515,961,000	605,072,000	−89,111,000	8.26%	1,436,701,000
1900	567,241,000	520,861,000	46,380,000	6.76%	1,263,417,000
1901	587,685,000	524,617,000	63,068,000	5.90%	1,221,572,000
1902	562,478,000	485,234,000	77,244,000	5.45%	1,178,031,000
1903	561,881,000	517,006,000	44,875,000	5.06%	1,159,406,000
1904	541,087,000	583,660,000	−42,573,000	4.96%	1,136,259,000
1905	544,275,000	567,279,000	−23,004,000	4.51%	1,132,357,000
1906	594,984,000	570,202,000	24,782,000	3.98%	1,142,523,000
1907	665,860,000	579,129,000	86,731,000	3.77%	1,147,178,000
1908	601,862,000	659,196,000	−57,334,000	4.25%	1,177,690,000

YEAR	REVENUES	OUTLAYS	ANNUAL SURPLUS (DEFICIT)	DEBT AS % OF GNP/GDP	ACCUMULATED NATIONAL DEBT
1909	604,320,000	693,744,000	−89,424,000	3.44%	1,148,315,000
1910	675,512,000	693,617,000	−18,105,000	3.25%	1,146,940,000
1911	701,833,000	691,202,000	10,631,000	3.22%	1,153,985,000
1912	692,609,000	689,881,000	2,728,000	3.03%	1,193,839,000
1913	714,463,000	714,864,000	−401,000	3.01%	1,193,048,000
1914	725,117,000	725,525,000	−408,000	3.08%	1,188,235,000
1915	683,417,000	746,093,000	−62,676,000	2.98%	1,191,264,000
1916	761,445,000	712,967,000	48,478,000	2.54%	1,225,146,000
1917	1,100,500,000	1,953,857,000	−853,357,000	4.93%	2,975,619,000
1918	3,645,240,000	12,677,359,000	−9,032,119,000	16.30%	12,455,225,000
1919	5,130,042,000	18,492,665,000	−13,362,623,000	30.34%	25,484,506,000
1920	6,648,898,000	6,357,677,000	291,221,000	26.56%	24,299,321,000
1921	5,570,790,000	5,061,785,000	509,005,000	34.45%	23,977,451,000
1922	4,025,901,000	3,289,404,000	736,497,000	30.99%	22,963,382,000
1923	3,852,795,000	3,140,287,000	712,508,000	26.26%	22,349,707,000
1924	3,871,214,000	2,907,847,000	963,367,000	25.09%	21,250,813,000
1925	3,640,805,000	2,923,762,000	717,043,000	22.04%	20,516,194,000
1926	3,795,108,000	2,929,964,000	865,144,000	20.25%	19,643,216,000
1927	4,012,794,000	2,857,429,000	1,155,365,000	19.51%	18,511,907,000
1928	3,900,329,000	2,961,245,000	939,084,000	18.15%	17,604,293,000
1929	3,861,589,000	3,127,199,000	734,390,000	16.42%	16,931,088,000
1930	4,057,884,000	3,320,211,000	737,673,000	17.90%	16,185,310,000
1931	3,115,557,000	3,577,434,000	−461,877,000	22.17%	16,801,281,000
1932	1,923,892,000	4,659,182,000	−2,735,290,000	33.60%	19,487,002,000
1933	1,996,844,000	4,598,496,000	−2,601,652,000	40.54%	22,538,673,000
1934	3,014,970,000	6,644,602,000	−3,629,632,000	41.56%	27,053,141,000
1935	3,705,956,000	6,497,008,000	−2,791,052,000	39.75%	28,700,893,000
1936	3,997,059,000	8,421,608,000	−4,424,549,000	40.94%	33,778,542,000
1937	4,955,613,000	7,733,033,000	−2,777,420,000	40.29%	36,424,614,000
1938	5,588,012,000	6,764,628,000	−1,176,616,000	43.88%	37,164,740,000
1939	4,979,066,000	8,841,224,000	−3,862,158,000	44.68%	40,439,532,000
1940	6,879,000,000	9,055,269,000	−2,176,269,000	50.85%	42,967,581,000
1941	9,202,000,000	13,254,948,000	−4,052,948,000	46.18%	48,961,444,000
1942	15,104,000,000	34,036,861,000	−18,932,861,000	50.16%	72,422,445,000
1943	25,097,000,000	79,867,714,000	−54,770,714,000	74.43%	135,895,090,000
1944	47,818,000,000	94,956,002,000	−47,138,002,000	97.14%	201,008,387,000
1945	50,162,000,000	98,802,937,000	−48,640,937,000	122.75%	258,682,187,000
1946	43,537,000,000	60,926,042,000	−17,389,042,000	129.98%	269,422,099,000

APPENDIX

YEAR	REVENUES	OUTLAYS	ANNUAL SURPLUS (DEFICIT)	DEBT AS % OF GNP/GDP	ACCUMULATED NATIONAL DEBT
1947	43,531,000,000	38,928,879,000	4,602,121,000	111.15%	258,286,383,000
1948	45,357,000,000	32,955,232,000	12,401,768,000	97.83%	252,292,247,000
1949	41,576,000,000	39,474,413,000	2,101,587,000	98.48%	252,770,360,000
1950	40,940,000,000	39,544,037,000	1,395,963,000	90.20%	257,357,352,000
1951	53,390,000,000	48,970,284,000	4,419,716,000	77.74%	255,221,977,000
1952	68,011,000,000	66,305,201,000	1,705,799,000	74.99%	259,105,179,000
1953	71,495,000,000	74,119,798,000	−2,624,798,000	72.96%	266,071,082,000
1954	69,719,000,000	70,889,744,000	−1,170,744,000	74.23%	271,259,599,000
1955	65,469,000,000	68,509,184,000	−3,040,184,000	68.94%	274,374,223,000
1956	74,547,000,000	70,460,329,000	4,086,671,000	65.08%	272,750,814,000
1957	79,990,000,000	76,740,583,000	3,249,417,000	61.75%	270,627,172,000
1958	79,636,000,000	82,575,095,000	−2,939,095,000	62.53%	276,845,218,000
1959	79,249,000,000	92,104,459,000	−12,855,459,000	59.50%	284,705,907,000
1960	92,492,000,000	92,223,354,000	268,646,000	57.75%	286,330,761,000
1961	94,389,000,000	97,794,579,000	−3,405,579,000	56.32%	288,970,989,000
1962	99,676,000,000	106,812,594,000	−7,136,594,000	54.13%	295,200,823,000
1963	106,560,000,000	111,311,144,000	−4,751,144,000	52.63%	305,859,633,000
1964	112,662,000,000	118,583,708,000	−5,921,708,000	50.09%	311,712,899,000
1965	116,833,000,000	118,429,745,000	−1,596,745,000	47.19%	317,273,899,000
1966	130,856,000,000	134,651,927,000	−3,795,927,000	43.94%	319,907,088,000
1967	149,552,000,000	158,254,257,000	−8,702,257,000	42.99%	326,220,985,000
1968	153,671,000,000	178,882,655,000	−25,211,655,000	42.79%	347,578,406,000
1969	187,784,000,000	184,556,043,000	3,227,957,000	39.46%	352,720,254,000
1970	193,743,000,000	196,587,786,000	−2,844,786,000	39.16%	370,918,707,000
1971	187,139,000,000	210,172,000,000	−23,033,000,000	38.38%	408,176,000,000
1972	207,309,000,000	230,681,000,000	−23,373,000,000	37.22%	435,936,000,000
1973	230,799,000,000	245,707,000,000	−14,908,000,000	35.69%	466,291,000,000
1974	263,224,000,000	269,359,000,000	−6,135,000,000	34.24%	483,893,000,000
1975	279,090,000,000	332,332,000,000	−53,242,000,000	35.74%	541,925,000,000
1976	298,060,000,000	371,792,000,000	−73,732,000,000	36.61%	628,970,000,000
1977	355,559,000,000	409,218,000,000	−53,659,000,000	36.83%	706,398,000,000
1978	399,561,000,000	458,746,000,000	−59,186,000,000	35.89%	776,602,000,000
1979	463,302,000,000	504,032,000,000	−40,729,000,000	34.28%	829,470,000,000
1980	517,112,000,000	590,947,000,000	−73,835,000,000	34.50%	909,050,000,000
1981	599,272,000,000	678,249,000,000	−78,976,000,000	33.84%	994,845,000,000
1982	617,766,000,000	745,755,000,000	−127,989,000,000	35.91%	1,137,345,000,000
1983	600,562,000,000	808,380,000,000	−207,818,000,000	40.26%	1,371,710,000,000
1984	666,457,000,000	851,846,000,000	−185,388,000,000	41.47%	1,564,657,000,000

YEAR	REVENUES	OUTLAYS	ANNUAL SURPLUS (DEFICIT)	DEBT AS % OF GNP/GDP	ACCUMULATED NATIONAL DEBT
1985	734,057,000,000	946,391,000,000	−212,334,000,000	45.31%	1,817,521,000,000
1986	769,091,000,000	990,336,000,000	−221,245,000,000	50.06%	2,120,629,000,000
1987	854,143,000,000	1,003,911,000,000	−149,769,000,000	51.67%	2,346,125,000,000
1988	908,954,000,000	1,064,140,000,000	−155,187,000,000	53.07%	2,601,307,000,000
1989	990,691,000,000	1,143,172,000,000	−152,481,000,000	54.68%	2,868,039,000,000
1990	1,031,321,000,000	1,252,705,000,000	−221,384,000,000	58.15%	3,206,564,000,000
1991	1,054,272,000,000	1,323,441,000,000	−269,169,000,000	63.45%	3,598,498,000,000
1992	1,090,453,000,000	1,380,856,000,000	−290,403,000,000	68.58%	4,002,136,000,000
1993	1,153,535,000,000	1,408,675,000,000	−255,140,000,000	68.60%	4,351,416,000,000
1994	1,257,745,000,000	1,460,914,000,000	−203,169,000,000	68.91%	4,643,711,000,000
1995	1,351,721,000,000	1,515,884,000,000	−163952000000	66.50%	4,920,586,000,000
1996	1,453,177,000,000	1,560,608,000,000	−107,431,000,000	66.20%	5,181,465,000,000
1997	1,579,423,000,000	1,601,307,000,000	−21,884,000,000	64.70%	5,369,206,000,000
1998	1,721,955,000,000	1,652,685,000,000	69,270,000,000	62.60%	5,478,189,000,000
1999	1,827,645,000,000	1,702,035,000,000	125,610,000,000	60.50%	5,605,523,000,000
2000	2,025,457,000,000	1,789,216,000,000	236,241,000,000	57.30%	5,628,700,000,000
2001	1,991,426,000,000	1,863,190,000,000	128,236,000,000	57.00%	5,769,881,000,000
2002	1,853,395,000,000	2,011,153,000,000	−157,758,000,000	59.20%	6,198,401,000,000
2003	1,782,532,000,000	2,160,117,000,000	−377,585,000,000	61.70%	6,760,014,000,000
2004	1,880,279,000,000	2,293,006,000,000	−412,727,000,000	62.90%	7,354,657,000,000
2005	2,153,859,000,000	2,472,205,000,000	−318,346,000,000	63.60%	7,905,300,000,000
2006	2,407,254,000,000	2,655,435,000,000	−248,181,000,000	64.10%	8,451,350,000,000
2007	2,568,239,000,000	2,730,241,000,000	−162,002,000,000	64.80%	8,950,744,000,000
2008	2,521,175,000,000	2,931,222,000,000	−410,047,000,000	67.70%	9,654,436,000,000
2009 est.	2,156,700,000,000	3,997,800,000,000	−1,420,000,000,000	81.54%	1,909,829,000,000

BIBLIOGRAPHY

Adams, Charles. *For Good and Evil: The Impact of Taxes on the Course of Civilization*. New York: Madison Books, 1993.

Bolles, Albert S. *The Financial History of the United States*. New York: Appleton, 1894.

Brewer, John. *The Sinews of Power: War, Money, and the English State, 1688–1783*. New York: Knopf, 1989.

Brimelow, Peter. "Not Yet." *Forbes*, July 19, 1993.

Buchanan, James M., and Richard E. Wagner. *Democracy in Deficit: The Political Legacy of Lord Keynes*. New York: Academic Press, 1977.

Carson, Gerald. *The Golden Egg: The Personal Income Tax: Where It Came From, How It Grew*. Boston: Houghton Mifflin, 1977.

Coffield, James. *A Popular History of Taxation: From Ancient to Modern Times*. London: Longman, 1970.

Cohn, Mary, ed. *Congressional Quarterly's Guide to Congress*. 4th ed. Washington, D.C.: Congressional Quarterly, 1991.

Cole, Al. "Presidents and Tax Reform." *Modern Maturity*, April–May, 1993.

Ferguson, E. James. *The Power of the Purse: A History of American Public Finance, 1776–1790*. Chapel Hill: University of North Carolina Press, 1961.

Hall, Robert E., and Alvin Rabushka. *The Flat Tax*. 2nd ed. Stanford, Calif.: Hoover Institution Press, 1995.

Hamilton, Alexander. *Papers on Public Credit, Commerce, and Finance*. New York: Columbia University Press, 1934.

Lee, Susan. *Hands Off: Why the Government Is a Menace to Economic Health*. New York: Simon and Schuster, 1996.

Malabre, Jr., Alfred L. *Beyond Our Means: How Reckless Borrowing Now Threatens to Overwhelm Us*. Paperback edition. New York: Vintage Books, 1988.

Mellon, Andrew. *Taxation: The People's Business*. New York: Macmillan, 1924.

Middlekauff, Robert. *The Glorious Cause: The American Revolution, 1763–1789*. New York: Oxford University Press, 1982.

Miller, John C. *Alexander Hamilton: Portrait in Paradox*. New York: Harper & Row, 1959.

Morris, Charles R. "It's Not the Economy, Stupid." *Atlantic Monthly*, July 1993.

Norton, Rob. "Our Screwed-Up Tax Code." *Fortune*, September 6, 1993.

O'Connor, Patricia Ann, ed. *Congress and the Nation*. Vol. 4, *1973–1976*. Washington, D.C.: Congressional Quarterly.

Ogilvie, Donald G. "Constitutional Limits and the Federal Budget." In Rudolph G. Penner, ed., *The Congressional Budget Process after Five Years*. Washington, D.C.: American Enterprise Institute for Public Policy Research, 1981.

Paul, Randolph E. *Taxation in the United States*. Boston: Little, Brown, 1954.

Remini, Robert V. *Andrew Jackson and the Bank War: A Study in the Growth of Presidential Power*. New York: Norton, 1967.

———. *Andrew Jackson and the Course of American Empire, 1767–1821*. (Vol. 1.) New York: Harper & Row, 1977.

———. *Andrew Jackson and the Course of American Freedom, 1822–1832*. (Vol. 2.) New York: Harper & Row, 1981.

———. *Andrew Jackson and the Course of American Democracy, 1833–1845*. (Vol. 3.) New York: Harper & Row, 1984.

Rothschild, Michael. *Bionomics: The Inevitability of Capitalism*. New York: Henry Holt, 1990.

Sapinsley, Barbara. *Taxes*. Issues in American History Series. New York: Franklin Watts, 1986.

Sinclair, David. *Dynasty: The Astors and Their Times*. New York: Beaufort Books, 1984.

Smith, Adam. *An Inquiry into the Nature and Causes of the Wealth of Nations*. New York: Modern Library, 1937 (a reprint of the fifth edition, 1789).

Witte, John F. *The Politics and Development of the Federal Income Tax*. Madison: University of Wisconsin Press, 1985.

INDEX

A NOTE ON THE AUTHOR

John Steele Gordon is one of America's leading historians specializing in business and financial history. He is the author of *An Empire of Wealth* and *The Great Game.* He has written for *Forbes, Worth,* the *New York Times,* the *Wall Street Journal,* and the *Washington Post.* John Steele Gordon lives in North Salem, New York.